Der Ball Ist Rund
EVERTON IN EUROPE
1962 - 2005

Mike Owen

First Published 2005 by Countyvise Limited,
14 Appin Road, Birkenhead, Wirral CH41 9HH.

Copyright © 2005 Mike Owen

The right of Mike Owen to be identified as the author of this work has been asserted by him in accordance with the Copyright, Design and Patents Act 1988.

The author has made every reasonable effort to contact all copyright holders. Any errors/omissions that may have occurred are inadvertent and regretted, and anyone who, for any reason, has not been contacted is invited to write to the publishers so that full acknowledgement may be made in subsequent editions of this work.

British Library Cataloguing in Publication Data.
A catalogue record for this book is available from the British Library.

Please note: From 1st January 2007 ISBNs will contain 13 numbers these numbers will be the same as the present number printed below the barcode (ie. starting 978).
Countyvise is showing both existing (10 digit) and future (13 digit) ISBNs on the Title page verso. Please continue to use the 10 figure number until 31st December 2006.

ISBN 1 901231 62 3   ISBN 978 1 901231 62 5

INTRODUCTION

I hope you find this footballing travelogue entertaining, enlightening and thought-provoking. Everton in Europe may seem a strange subject for a book. But it is a colourful strand of the rich tapestry of Everton history - a strand that is usually overlooked.

Librarians may wish to file this book under Mysteries. I had never understood why England's fourth most successful club - in terms of championships and FA Cups - had not fared better in Europe, particularly in the Harry Catterick years. Before our Cup Winners Cup triumph in 1985, as many as 12 different English clubs had won a European trophy but we had never even got past the quarter-finals.

Intrigued, I set out on an odyssey to write a chapter on each two-legged tie we have played, plus of course the 1985 final. Each chapter sheds light on the background of our opponents and strives to place the game within the context of the challenges Everton were facing at that time.

So why have Everton not done better in Europe? There are many issues to consider as you make your way through the book. Financial factors can be cited these days, but that was not what stopped us in the 1960s, nor in 1971 when we were one of the favourites to win the European Cup.

Many factors came into play, not least a very simple one: Der Ball Ist Rund. It's German for the The Ball Is Round. A famous phrase among football fans in Deutschland, it was coined by Sepp Herberger, coach of the West German team of part-timers and amateurs which defeated the legendary Hungarian team in the 1954 World Cup final. What he meant was that the ball can roll either way, don't be surprised in football, anything can happen, take nothing for granted.

It seemed an apt title for the book, given the narrow margin of many of our defeats. Also, Everton have enjoyed more success over clubs from Germany than any other nation in European competition. It's a topical title too, with Germany the venue for the 2006 World Cup finals.

As with any historical work, no matter how hard an author attempts to be objective, and sometimes I don't even try, the words are tinted by the writer's background and perspective of events. So I should state that I was born in September 1956 and saw my first Everton game in April 1963. I was brought up in Wirral on an overspill housing estate in Eastham, less than a mile from the River Mersey and six miles from Birkenhead. All my schoolmates supported either Everton or Liverpool, and Tranmere was our second team. Due to what may be termed the Shankly and Kop factors, there were probably two Reds to every Blue.

It was my original intention that the book should contain no mention whatsoever of Liverpool FC. For my life has been blighted by them. I sometimes wish we had just agreed to the rent rise in 1892 and then they might never have existed.

But to be honest, part of the inspiration for the book came from Liverpool supporters. It was all the arguments I had over the years. You know what it's like. For once you are winning an argument with them, you've got them on the back foot and they come back with their tedious, stand-by line: "Well how many times have you won the Eurovision Song Contest then?"

The more research I put into the book, the closer I came to the conclusion that if one wishes to offer some analysis of the development of Everton Football Club over the last 50 years, then we cannot view the Blues in isolation from rival clubs, especially Liverpool, nor in isolation from the Littlewoods business. Consequently, there is weaved into the book a thin thread relating to the company's founder, John Moores, and his family.

The book is the product of research carried out over two years into not only Everton but also the clubs we played. There was a wealth of material on the internet. Then there were many books to flick through again or read for the first time. A bibliography can be found at the back of the book. I also referred to match programmes and a multitude of newspaper articles from local and national publications, not least the Liverpool Echo, traditionally the first port of call for supporters seeking news of the Blues.

But best of all, I spoke to players who had taken part in some of these games. It was a great thrill for me to talk to former Everton players. The conversations were heart-warming for two reasons. Brian Labone, Alex Parker, Mike Pejic, Billy Wright, Derek Mountfield, Dai Davies and George Wood had enjoyed careers spanning hundreds of games yet they displayed unfailing courtesy to a stranger asking them if they could remember a handful of games from decades ago. The second uplifting feature was the passion conveyed in their voices for Everton; the club still clearly means a lot to them.

Spending an hour with Brian Labone, I could not help thinking it was a shame that this bright, sociable man who played 530 games for Everton and 26 times for England was never appointed a director of the club. It is what might have happened in Germany.

A special mention of George Wood too. I still chuckle when I recall ringing him on his mobile phone and explaining the nature of my call. Hearing the sound of running water in the background, I asked him if it was an inconvenient time to speak? Was he running a bath? "No," he replied earnestly. "I'm standing in a river." I then remembered all those interviews he gave in the Seventies and how he was a keen angler.

I have written my own account of the games, drawing on all the aforementioned sources and, in some cases, the recollections of myself and other Evertonians.

Next, may I explain that this book has been produced independently. The standard practice is for an author to seek a publisher who will look after printing, distribution, marketing and sales. But I thought they would laugh me out of their office if I told them I was writing a book about Everton in Europe. So I did it my way. I asked Birkenhead Press to print the book. Not only would it be made on Merseyside, but I knew they had done an excellent job of producing, Cien Años de Calidad, La Historia de Everton Football Club, written in Spanish by the Ruleteros Society. And their printworks is overlooked by the house in which my dad John was born and spent his early years, in Hinderton Road, Tranmere. He died, aged 77, in 2002 and I still miss him and this is an opportune place to thank my mum Lily for sewing a number 9 on my back all those years ago so I could pretend I was Fred Pickering.

Some readers may be disappointed that there are no photographs in the book. All I can say is: Did Shakespeare have photos in his books? Did Dickens? No! The words in this book evoke pictures in the mind. Actually, I would have liked to have included some interesting photographs, but they are not easy to obtain and all my time was taken up with the text.

Similarly, the statisticians may be a little disappointed. But I wanted it to be a story book. So you will find 25 chapters giving 25 separate stories which link together to give a fresh, sometimes a little surreal, perspective on this wonderful football club.

With the book featuring clubs from Scotland, Italy, Norway, Germany, Hungary, Denmark, Spain, Iceland, Greece, Ireland, the Czech Republic, Holland, Slovakia, Austria and Romania, I would like it to be seen as an Evertonian contribution to our home city's year as European Capital of Culture 2008.

Finally, a series of thanks. To my wife Gill, who thinks I love Everton more than her, for putting up with me writing the book. To Gerry Allison for translating articles from the Heraldo de Aragon newspaper on the Real Zaragoza games in 1966 and to Paul Preston for obtaining those reports. Similarly, I must thank "Curly" Prins for translating the history of Fortuna Sittard. And I am indebted to Alan Rigg, Peter Hill, John Shearon, Tony Heslop, Tony Bethel, Peter Hill and Brian Williamson for proof-reading and feedback. Thanks also to George Orr, Teresa McMullen, Donny MacKechnie, Steve Parker, Tony O'Neill and Peter Barnes for taking the time to talk to me about their recollections. I did intend to talk to more people, but pressures of time got the better of me. However, I can do that for the second edition, after we have played again in Europe. Thanks for miscellaneous help to Vicki & Dennis Fogarty, Tom & Jack Owen, Brian Hartley and Ian MacDonald. Finally, if you have bought his book, thank you. I hope to be able to make a donation to the Former Players' Foundation and to the Everton (David France) Collection Charitable Trust.

Mike Owen
October 2005

CONTENTS

1. IT ALL KICKS OFF

Dunfermline
Inter Cities Fairs Cup
1962-63

THE spectre of World War Three loomed over Goodison Park as Everton prepared for their first game in European competition. It was Wednesday 24th October 1962 and mankind feared that it was teetering on the brink of a nuclear holocaust. Even the Number One hit single in Britain that day conjured up images of missiles hurtling through the air - Telstar, by the Tornados.

Just two days earlier American President John F. Kennedy had told his nation that the Soviet Union was building secret missile bases in Cuba, 90 miles from the Florida coast. He demanded that the Russians remove the bases and he ordered a naval blockade of Cuba to prevent Soviet ships from delivering more missiles and construction materials. In return Russian Premier Nikita Khrushchev ordered his commanders in Cuba to launch their tactical nuclear weapons at the United States if the Caribbean isle was invaded by America. The world was scared. Around 40,000 Evertonians did what they knew best - they went to watch the Blues at Goodison Park.

Everton were playing Dunfermline in the Inter Cities Fairs Cup. As the supporters walked up the streets leading to the ground, many hoped that the game would take their minds of the Cuban Missile Crisis and the threat of a nuclear holocaust. It certainly did that. For the two teams played as if it was the last game of their lives and the visitors, if not the home team too, took no prisoners. According to some of those present, it was one of the dirtiest games ever seen at Goodison Park.

Certainly, it was not what Evertonians had been led to expect from the relatively new phenomenon of European club football. British fans had slowly but surely been taking an increasing interest in the game overseas. This had been kickstarted by the great Hungary team which had thrashed England 6-3 at Wembley in 1953 and further fuelled when many saw on television the 1960 European Cup final in which Real Madrid beat Eintracht Frankfurt 7-3 in what was thought to be one of the greatest games ever.

So when Everton entered the 1962-63 Fairs Cup there was considerable excitement at whom the Blues may draw: Barcelona, Roma, Marseille, Porto, Ferencvaros and Sampdoria were among the 32 teams in the hat. Instead, we drew Dunfermline. "A blinking Scottish team," said Alex Parker who played right-back for Everton in both legs. "We were all laughing, especially as half of our team were Scottish."

Qualifying for the Fairs Cup was one of the first signs that Everton were finally emerging from a prolonged post-war slump. Not since 1939 had Everton won a trophy when Tommy Lawton's goals helped the Blues win the last championship before the outbreak of the Second World War. By the time the Football League resumed in 1946, Lawton had been sold to Chelsea and Everton finished the first post-war season in 10th place. Remarkably, the Blues failed to finish in the top ten again until 1961.

This was one year after Littlewoods tycoon John Moores had become chairman in summer 1960 when it was revealed at the club's annual general meeting that some months earlier he had made the club an interest-free loan of £56,000. Moores had told the AGM: "Everton must have the best players, the best coaches, the best manager and the best directors. If any of them fail, they must go."

Consequently, the pressure was on Johnny Carey as the 1960-61 season began, his third as manager at Goodison. When Christmas arrived, Evertonians were walking in a Carey Wonderland, third in the table, challenging for the championship for the first time in more than 20 years. But after beating the champions Burnley on Boxing Day, the Blues suffered five successive league defeats. We also went out of the FA Cup in the 3rd round. Carey managed to arrest the slide, keeping us in the top six. Everton then had a good Easter, winning two games and drawing one, before going up to Newcastle and winning 4-0. It left us fifth in the table, with three games to go. Carey was stunned when he was sacked a few days later.

His successor was Harry Catterick. Yet 18 months later when Everton took the field against Dunfermline in the Fairs Cup, there were only three players whom Catterick had introduced to the team: goalkeeper Gordon West, bought from Blackpool, inside right Dennis Stevens, signed from Bolton, and left-winger Johnny Morrissey, plucked from Liverpool reserves. The other players were Alex Parker, signed from Falkirk by Carey's predecessor Ian Buchan; local lads Brian Labone and Brian Harris who had risen through the youth ranks; and five players bought in 1960 by Carey: Roy Vernon, Jimmy Gabriel, Billy Bingham, George Thomson and Alex Young.

Dunfermline were very much an unknown quantity but their manager was to become legendary. Jock Stein was reserve team coach at Celtic when he was asked in 1960 to take charge of a Dunfermline team facing relegation. Under his command, they won their last five games of the season to narrowly avoid the drop. Little did the Dunfermline supporters know that their club, nicknamed the Pars, was about to embark on its greatest ever period.

With Dunfermline being a small city with a population of around 45,000, its football club had ever since its formation in 1885 been overshadowed by the bigger clubs 20 miles away in Edinburgh and further to the west in Glasgow. But Stein did not see any reason to stay in their shadows. George Peebles, who played in both games against Everton, recalled: "When Jock first took over he gathered all the players together and told us we were better than we thought. He said we should be wanting to play the Real Madrids and the Eintrachts. We were due to play Cowdenbeath on the Saturday and all the boys looked at each other and thought, "Who is he trying to kid?" Two years later we were all boarding a flight to Spain to play Valencia in the Fairs Cup."

Steins's first full season ended with the club reaching the Scottish Cup final where they faced Celtic in front of 120,000 people - more than double the population of Dunfermline. Celtic had won the Cup 17 times, Dunfermline not once. The game ended in a goalless draw and the teams returned to Hampden the following Wednesday. Dunfermline won 2-0, putting them into the draw for the European Cup Winners Cup of 1961-62 in which Stein's team beat St Patricks of Dublin and Yugoslav cup winners Vardar Skopje before going out in the quarter-finals to Ujpest Dozsa of Hungary. The six games gave Dunfermline experience of European competition, something that Everton lacked.

Just like Everton, Dunfermline had finished fourth in the league in 1962 to qualify for the Fairs Cup. Peebles said: "Dunfermline were just a workmanlike side but Stein had us all doing our jobs and we were a difficult side to beat."

That was to become painfully clear to Evertonians, including the teenage George Orr, a Blue who later recalled: "Dunfermline came to kick us off the park. They treated it as if it was a Scottish international against England. They kicked Everton apart because Everton were a skilful team although they could mix it."

The game started innocuously enough but it soon became clear that Dunfermline would be content with a draw as they sat back. Everton took the lead midway through the first half when a Bingham corner was met at the near post by Stevens whose back header hit the underside of the crossbar and bounced downwards. The defender Jim McLean hacked it clear, but the Dublin referee Meighan ruled that the ball had bounced over the line. His decision put Stevens in the history books as the scorer of Everton's first goal in European competition.

The controversial nature of the goal may have angered the Dunfermline players. Certainly, the level of aggression in the game escalated after that. It was always going to be hardly fought, if only because of the Anglo-Scots rivalry which was intense in the 1960s. However the tackles began flying in with greater intensity, leading to players squaring up to each other on several occasions.

When the second half began, Everton were forced into a change. Thomson had sustained an injury, said to be to his thigh, that rendered him too slow to play his normal role at full back. There were no substitutions in those days so he spent the second half as a limping outside left. Dunfermline continued to concentrate on sitting back, but occasionally would break away sharply and threaten the Everton defence. Labone had to throw in a last-gasp tackle to stop George Miller and Harris cleared a Dan McLindon header off the line.

Everton huffed and puffed as they tried to break down the Dunfermline defence which had Roy Vernon and Alex Young well shackled. The Blues alternated between patiently knocking the ball around in midfield, waiting for an opening to appear, and impatiently hoofing it long. When the Blues did get a shot in on goal, the Dunfermline keeper Jim Herriot was in fine form.

There were no goals in the second half, which left Everton with a 1-0 win. The Dunfermline team was booed off the pitch. The next day in the Liverpool Echo and Evening Express, Leslie Edwards described the game as a "miserable exhibition". He added: "The odd handshakes at the end - what a hypocritical gesture! - must have been mutual congratulations between players who were able to walk off on two sound legs."

The newspaper's letters column was later packed with suggestions from angry Evertonians. One complained that he had paid three shillings for a football match but all he saw was a public brawl. Another suggested that Everton should select their reserves for the return match; another wanted the RAF to be sent. However one said the Everton team had a reputation for "toughness", citing three games in which the Blues had stood up for themselves. These were "friendlies" against Hibs and the touring Brazilian team Bangu, plus an FA Cup tie against Kings Lynn.

One of the players who took part in the Dunfermline game, Parker, denied that it was dirty. "It was just a hard game," he said. "Jock Stein was a hard man, a nice man but a hard taskmaster. He was just starting out in management. I played against him when he was at Celtic and I was at Falkirk. He was a big, hard centre-half who took no prisoners."

The return leg was the following Wednesday. In between, Everton had a home game against champions Ipswich whose manager Alf Ramsey had just announced he would be leaving the club at the end of the season to take over as manager of England, succeeding

Walter Winterbottom. During a first half played in steady drizzle, Everton took the lead against Ipswich with a penalty from Vernon. It poured down at half time and, on all four sides of Goodison Park, the spectators on the terraces moved backwards to shelter under the stands, giving the ground an empty appearance. Ipswich equalised on 53 minutes but with just quarter of an hour to go Morrissey scored twice in a minute to give Everton a 3-1 win. It was a great confidence booster for the players as they looked towards the second leg of the Fairs Cup tie.

And on the Sunday, the world was able to relax. After seven days of deadlock between the two nuclear superpowers, Kruschev stood back from the brink, ordering all Soviet supply ships away from Cuban waters and agreeing to remove the missiles from Cuba's mainland.

It was only on the day of the second-leg that Everton set off for the game, and with just 14 players. The team that had played on Saturday, plus Albert Dunlop, Frank Heslop and Frank Wignall, boarded a plane at Speke Airport, on the southern outskirts of Liverpool. They were accompanied on the flight to Edinburgh by directors Cyril Balmforth and Holland Hughes and club secretary Bill Dickinson. From Edinburgh, there was a 30-minute journey by road to Dunfermline, a city proud of its historic abbey and of being the burial place of Robert the Bruce.

Stein was ready and waiting, having told reporters that morning: "We recognise Everton are a great team. The lessons learned in the first leg will form the basis of the plan to win tonight. Dunfermline can and will win."

When Stein won the European Cup with Celtic in 1967, beating Inter Milan 2-1 in the final in Lisbon, it was with a team of players who all hailed from within around 30 miles of Glasgow. This had echoes of his achievements at Dunfermline where he took a bunch of footballers, most of whom came from within a radius of 30 miles or little more, and moulded them into a formidable force that could compete with the best in Europe.

No Everton player was looking forward to the second leg more than Parker. "I was made up to be going home," he said. "I had a lot of people I knew coming across from my former club Falkirk to watch. I remember there was the trainer and a few of the players."

One of Catterick's big hopes must have been that we did not concede an early goal, but that was dashed when the Pars' left-half Miller hit a volley from 20 yards. West got his fingers to the ball but could not stop it nestling in the back of the net. It was 1-1 on aggregate. Everton were playing poorly while Stein's team knocked the ball around neatly. Dunfermline played with five at the back but, with the bulk of the 21,000 crowd roaring them on, they pressed forward at every opportunity. The Pars nearly scored a second when Miller sent in another powerful shot but Harris blocked it on the line.

In the second half Everton played much better after Catterick made a change to the tactics although there was an oversight. Parker said: "I don't have too much recollection of the game itself but I do remember that we had set ourselves out a plan, a formation to play, and that in the first half I had diarrhoea. So as soon as I got in at half-time I went in the toilet. I was in there for the whole of the break until they started banging and shouting at me to go out for the second half. I'm playing away and unbeknown to me they had changed the tactics. No-one had said a word to me. It was halfway through the second half before I got to know."

The second half was said to be an entertaining affair, with Gabriel outstanding in midfield. Hard-working, good at winning the ball and adept at getting forward into goalscoring positions, Gabriel had three chances in the second half. The first brought a brilliant save from Herriot soon after the break, the second was a header which eluded the keeper but was cleared by a defender, while the third was a shot that forced another save from Herriot. As the minutes ticked way, with the aggregate score 1-1, it looked increasingly likely that the two teams would have to go to a third game on a neutral ground.

With just three or four minutes left Everton were attacking, looking for the winner, when Willie Cunningham managed to win the ball from Morrissey. The Pars captain played a long ball for Harry Melrose who looked three yards offside. The linesman's flag went up but the referee did not blow. Melrose raced towards goal and, as West came out, the Scot slipped the ball past him. The place erupted. Melrose was surrounded by his teammates who tumbled to the floor in their delight. Everton players persuaded the Belfast referee Carswell to talk to the linesman but he did not change his decision.

It was 2-0 on the night and 2-1 on aggregate to Dunfermline. We needed a late equaliser to take the tie to a play-off. Bingham put a cross over that caused panic in the Dunfermline defence and Young put the ball in the net, reeling away in delight. But the referee ruled that Morrissey had committed a handball and disallowed it. Everton were out.

In the next round, Dunfermline were drawn against the holders of the trophy, Valencia, who comfortably won the first leg in Spain 4-0. It looked all over but on a cold December night Dunfermline won the return leg 6-2, to make it 6-6 on aggregate. It went to a play-off two months later in Lisbon where Valencia won 1-0. The Spaniards went on to retain the Fairs Cup. But Evertonians also had plenty to celebrate at the end of the season.

2. DAUGHTER TERESA

Inter Milan
European Cup
1963-64

In 1963 Everton won their first trophy since the 1930s, running away with the championship to become England's entrants for the European Cup. The Blues could have drawn a star-studded Real Madrid, including Di Stefano and Puskas, who had won the first five European Cups. Or they might have been pitted against Benfica who had won the trophy in 1961 and 1962. Instead the Blues got an even tougher draw. Inter Milan were about to embark on the greatest run the proud Italian club has ever known, before or since. Having won Serie A in 1963, they were to repeat the feat in 1965 and 1966. But more impressively, Inter were to win not only the European Cup in two successive seasons, but also the Inter Continental Cup - better known as the world club championship – in consecutive years.

Their game was based on superb defending and slick passing that allowed them to counter attack at pace. It was becoming the trademark of Italian football and there were no better exponents than Inter Milan, coached by Helenio Herrera, an Argentinian who had previously taken Barcelona to glory. What's more, these guys were so classy they also had fantastic names, such as Giacinto Facchetti and Sandro Mazzola. There was always great sympathy for the latter because his father Valentino had been killed in the 1949 plane crash which wiped out a great Torino team.

British football fans had little first-hand knowledge of Italian club football and there was a great atmosphere in the city on the day of the game. The Beatles had just gone to Number One in the charts with She Loves You and there was a tremendous air of anticipation surrounding the visit of Inter. George Orr said: "It was chaos before the game. I was working in T.J. Hughes in London Road and the city centre was blocked because the traffic was horrendous going up to Goodison. I have never seen the likes of it since. It was as if everyone was going to the game earlier than normal. It was pandemonium trying to get to the ground."

It was the first European Cup match to take place on Merseyside. Ticket prices had been raised for the game but there was still a 62,000 crowd, which included several hundred Italians. "They had brought a flag 30ft or 40ft long that was draped right along one of the stands and there was a tremendous atmosphere inside the ground," recalled Orr. Indeed, to coin a phrase, it was one of the great European nights at Goodison. In fact, it was the first great European night on Merseyside. The Everton team was: West, Parker, Harris, Gabriel, Labone, Kay, Scott, Stevens, Young, Vernon, Temple.

Tony Kay had been bought from Sheffield Wednesday for £55,000 and Alex Scott from Glasgow Rangers for £40,000. This had led the newspaper headline writers to describe Everton as the Mersey Millionaires. But Moores had not paid for the players out of his own pocket. He had made the club an interest-free loan of £100,000, it had emerged at the club's annual general meeting in June 1963.

The idea that Moores was donating money to the club may well have arose because the loans went down in the accounts under donations, and the club accounts were published some weeks before they were explained in some detail at the AGM by director Holland Hughes, chairman of the club's finance committee. After the AGM, Moores told reporters: "The directors would not agree to having these players unless I put up the money. This was my biggest loan to the club."

Inter were largely in control in the first half with their goalkeeper Giuliano Sarti rarely troubled. Some might have said Everton were a little in awe of them. Others might have said that the visitors' ball control and passing was simply a cut above. Horst Szymaniak covered every blade of grass while Spain's inside left Luis Suarez was showing all his skill and passing ability but possibly the most dangerous was the Brazilian winger Jair da Costa. At the back, centre-half Aristide Guarneri was magnificient and mainly in control of Alex Young. Roy Vernon was almost marked out of the game by Carlo Tagnin. Nor was there any way down the wings for Everton as the Inter fullbacks Tarcisio Burgnich and Facchetti showed all the cunning and class that made them Italian internationals.

Orr said: "That 1963 team is still the best Everton team for me, for all-round skill and ability. But that Inter Milan team was incredible. It was the first time I had seen a football team and thought this is a machine. Everton and the other top team of the time, Tottenham, had tactics but they played more free-flowing, off the cuff. With Inter, I saw an organisation we had never seen before in football. It was like a Rolls Royce, it was purring, everything was planned - and a lot of it was geared to stopping the other team from scoring."

This had a lot to do with the coaching of Herrera, credited by many with introducing the sweeper system. He had been a big success at Barcelona, taking them to two championships and two Fairs Cups triumphs before committing the cardinal sin of losing to Real Madrid in a European Cup semi-final. After leaving Barcelona, he received several offers and plumped for Inter.

Everton did manage however to create opportunities against Inter at Goodison, with shots coming in from Vernon, Brian Harris and Alex Parker. The fierce-tackling Kay was stamping his mark on the game - and on the hand of Suarez, a misdemeanour which earned him a booking. Parker was Everton's right back but he had no left-sided attacking player to mark, which allowed him to make frequent forays into the Inter half. He recalled: "I did that much running in that game I lost six or seven pounds. I was knackered. I had a very good chance but the keeper saved it."

Inter counter-attacked with pace and precision, creating three or four chances for Jair who put his shots wide although there was one occasion when Everton had Harris to thank for a timely tackle. In the second half Everton stepped up the pressure and played with more authority. Dennis Stevens, Vernon and Young all had chances with headers - two went over the bar, only the Scot's required a save from Sarti.

Time was beginning to run out for the Blues when, in the 80th minute, Stevens prodded the ball forward in the penalty box for Vernon who poked it into the net and the crowd jumped in delight, until they saw the referee disallowing it for offside. To this day, Brian Labone believes it was a good goal. Jimmy Gabriel, who had been pushed forward into attack in the second half, flashed a header over the bar. The Inter defence had been pressed on to its back foot but this was something with which they were comfortable. The game finished goalless, but the crowd knew they had seen a special team and applauded the Italians off the pitch.

The return leg was just a week later. On the day before the game, around 140 Evertonians flew from Speke to Milan on two chartered planes, a Starways DC4 and a Viscount, which also contained an 8ft-wide photocopy of a Good Luck telegram the supporters had sent to the team. Among the passengers was 21-year-old Teresa McMullen. Now aged in her 60s she has lived all her life in Merseyside but 40 years later it was still the only Everton game she had attended.

She explained: "My dad was a fanatical Evertonian but he was very ill at the time and there was no way he could get on a plane. I really felt for him so I said 'Shall I go for you, dad?' His eyes went all watery. That was it, I was going. My sister Bernadette said she'd come too and we paid £11 each for our tickets. My dad was thrilled to bits because it made up for him not going. There'd be a little bit of him there and we'd come back and tell him all about it. But then my sister had to cancel because she had a nursing exam. My dad was worried about me going on my own and I was very nervous about it, I would not know a soul on the trip, but I wanted to do it for him. I turned up at Speke Airport and saw all these fellas and thought to myself, 'What have I let myself in for?'"

Milan is similar to the city of Liverpool in that it has two proud football clubs, with the second emerging from a bitter row in the early years of the first.

The bust-up in North-West England's premier city was over money. The landlord of Everton's Anfield ground, John Houlding, wanted more rent, the club refused and went to Goodison. Houlding was left with a football ground and no team so he set about hastily assembling one. But who was going to support this team? Most local football enthusiasts had been supporting Everton. Fortunately for Houlding the game's appeal was growing; the name of his new team would be important. What better than Liverpool, with which people throughout the city could identify? It was a good marketing ploy. With one of the best grounds in the country and a team bearing the name of England's Second City, Houlding succeeded in getting Liverpool admitted to the Football League within just a year.

The bust-up in North-West Italy's premier city was political. The Milan Cricket and Football Club, now better known as AC Milan, was set up in 1899 and soon won three Italian championships. But in March 1908, a group of rebels, unhappy about a ban on foreigners playing for the club, broke away to form Internazionale Milano.

Captained by a Swiss player, Hernst Manktl, Internazionale began playing in gold, black and blue, the colours that are still worn today. They soon achieved success, winning the title in 1910; a second Scudetto followed in 1920. After the Fascist dictator Benito Mussolini took over, Internazionale were forced to merge with the Milanese Unione Sportiva and won three Scudettos under the name of Ambrosiana Inter, in 1930, 1938 and 1940. The club's first Coppa Italia success came in 1939. After the fall of Mussolini, the name Ambrosiana was abandoned and the club returned to its previous name. It won the Scudetto in 1953 and 1954, and in 1963.

The game at the San Siro is best known in Everton history as the debut of Colin Harvey who went on to play almost 400 games for the Blues before later becoming manager. However it perhaps serves foremost for illustrating the thin line that exists between success and failure. If Everton could have scored the only goal of the two-legged tie, and they certainly had the chances, then they might well have progressed to the 1964 European Cup final in Vienna and met Real Madrid. Indeed, the second leg of this first-round tie was actually played as if a place in the final was at stake. No prisoners were taken in a match punctuated by ugly fouls and personal battles. The Everton team was: West, Parker, Harris, Stevens, Labone, Kay, Scott, Harvey, Young, Vernon, Temple.

It was a game that Teresa nearly missed. She said: "I seem to remember we had a good flight and it was good fun. There were one or two other women there, but because I was on my own, and I was a young 21, I think everyone thought they had to look after me. I think we must have been delayed because I know I didn't get to my bedroom. I just remember us all sitting in the hotel on these sofas and easy chairs. We had a sightseeing tour of Milan as part of the trip and I think it was going very early. So we must have thought it wasn't worth going to bed.

"Later we were all ready to go to the San Siro when I could not find my ticket for the game. I was distraught, thinking about my dad. Well, there was about five lads who acted as my guardian angels. They said, 'We've worked out a plan, we are going to smuggle you in. You get into the middle of us and we will carry you through the gates in the swell.' I thought, 'Oh no, I am going to get arrested and end up in prison.' Well, it was very busy at the San Siro and probably less stringent then than now. I can remember being pushed in between them as they very cleverly got me through. When we got inside the stadium, the atmosphere was absolutely electrifying."

The team had been staying at Monza, the town famous for its Grand Prix racetrack, and the players had been out for a stroll. "Every driver seemed to think he was Juan Fangio (a former world motor-racing champion)," recalled Labone. He added: "It was the days when British footballers had steaks for lunch before a game which, I think they say now, is one of the hardest things to digest. The hotel staff were trying to help us, offering us all this spaghetti and pasta. We thought they were trying to Mickey Finn us so we all stuck to our fillet steaks."

If that meal was anything like the Everton performance in the San Siro, it would have been superb. Teenage novice Harvey emerged from the game with praise ringing in his ears, although it could have been a nightmare debut as he played a back pass from 25 yards out that was intercepted by Di Giacomo. The Italian centre forward was so surprised to receive the ball that he rushed his shot and put it wide. However Harvey won plaudits for his enterprise in trying two shots with his back to goal. Some thought that Young played too deep to inflict damage on the Inter defence. Scott went on one brilliant 30-yard run past several Inter players, putting himself in a great position but from 12 yards out he fired wide.

The only goal of the game came just a minute into the second half when Tagnin pushed the ball through for Jair and although the angle seemed a difficult one the Brazilian rifled the ball into the top of the net. Parker puts the Inter goal down to a momentary loss of collective concentration during a highly committed performance by the Blues. More than 40 years on, Parker's voice winced as he recalled the moment of imperfection. "We were very unfortunate not to get a result. We only relaxed once and it was in the second half. They got a free kick near the halfway line. We just relaxed for a couple of seconds and one of their players pushed it out to Jair on the right wing and that was it. We never relaxed for more than those two seconds in the whole game, but we were still getting set up and we paid dearly for it."

After Inter's 1-0 win, which of course made the aggregate score 1-0, Herrera said: "Everton were bound to play this game defensively as we did at Goodison Park and until the interval I wasn't sure whether they were going to succeed or not."

In the following rounds Inter beat on aggregate Monaco 4-1, Partizan Belgrade 4-1, and Borussia Dortmund 4-2. Inter won five of those six games; they were held to a 2-2 draw in Germany. In the final, a Real Madrid team that included legendary players such as Santamaria, Amancio, Di Stefano, Puskas and Gento lost 3-1 to Inter in front of a crowd of 74,000 in Austria. Then Inter beat the Argentine club Independiente over three legs, a play-off was needed, to establish themselves as world club champions. They repeated the feat the following season, retaining both the European Cup and the world club championship.

Against Dunfermline and Milan, we had gone out of European competition at the first hurdle, in each case by one goal. We had argued that the Scots' late winner should have been disallowed for offside. While in the first leg against Inter, it was felt that an effort by Vernon should not have been disallowed for offside. Such is the thin line between success and failure.

3. A QUIFF LIKE ELVIS

Valerengen
Inter Cities Fairs Cup
1964-65

After the heartache in Milan, Everton went close to retaining the championship. In March 1964 the Blues were top of the league, with just five games to go. But in the next four games we picked up just one point and finished third, five points behind Liverpool, who won their first title since 1947. It meant the Blues and Reds had each won six titles each. We qualified for the Inter Cities Fairs Cup, along with Manchester United who had finished second.

Everton were drawn to play an Oslo XI that would draw on players from several clubs in the Norwegian capital and represent the city in accordance with the original ethos of the competition. But one of those clubs, Skeid Oslo, had entered the Cup Winners Cup and another, FK Lyn, the European Cup. If players from those clubs were also required for two games in the Fairs Cup, arrangements could get complicated. As a result, Valerengen were asked to represent Norway in the Fairs Cup.

Before our flight to Oslo there was the little matter of a derby match. We went to Anfield on the back of five league games without a win. Blues supporters were understandably a little pessimistic. It turned out to be one of the greatest derbies ever. We thrashed them 4-0 with goals from Colin Harvey, Johnny Morrissey, Derek Temple and Fred Pickering. "Big Fred" was establishing himself as a firm favourite with Blues fans. He had been signed in March from Blackburn for £85,000, scored a hat-trick on his debut and a total of nine goals in the last nine games of the season. His goal at Anfield was his eighth in the first nine games of the new season - 17 goals in his first 18 league games, and he had a quiff like Elvis.

Notably though, after July 1964 - when we signed Ray Wilson from Huddersfield in exchange for £35,000 and Mick Meagan - the rate of signings slowed considerably. During the rest of the Sixties, Everton only made three big signings - £110,000 for Alan Ball in 1966 and £80,000 each for Ernie Hunt and Howard Kendall in 1967 - until the last month of the decade when we bought Keith Newton for £80,000.

The game in Oslo was Pickering's first taste of European club football. Valerengen had been formed in 1913, but had never won the Norwegian championship, even though clubs from northern Norway were excluded, due to the problems at that time of travelling long distances in a mountainous country. It was to be another seven years or so before there was a fully national league.

There was a crowd of 18,000 in Oslo to see the famous English side. Everton fielded the team that had conquered Anfield. In the opening minutes Pickering hit the post but the game was scoreless for the first quarter. When a goal was scored, it came from Valerengen after Brian Labone fouled Leif Eriksen in the 27th minute and the Swedish referee pointed to the penalty spot. Local hero Bruno Larsen converted. Pickering soon put Everton level and at half-time it was 1-1.

But just a minute into the second half the home side took the lead again following a mistake by Labone which allowed Larsen to pass to Eriksen who fired home from 10 yards out. A shock appeared to be on the cards as the Norwegians battled manfully. But in the 70th minute Alex Scott crossed and Pickering headed an equaliser. A 2-2 draw would have been sufficient, if not satisfactory, for Everton to take back to Goodison for the second leg. But the superior fitness of the full-timers came into play and Everton scored three in the last 12 minutes. Harvey latched on to a loose ball in the 78th minute and powered it home to put Everton ahead for the first time in the game. Six minutes later, Temple added another. In the dying seconds Scott made it 5-2.

The following Saturday Big Fred netted twice as Everton won 5-3 at Birmingham. It was a good week's work for the Blues - 14 goals in three away wins, with Pickering scoring five. Evertonians were happy and the Number One single was the Herman's Hermits feel-good song I'm Into Something Good.

The Inter Cities Fairs Cup, later renamed the UEFA Cup, was winning increasing respect as a competition among Europe's leading clubs, probably because it was gradually becoming a competition where entry was based on merit. This was the first season that England's entrants were the teams that had finished immediately behind the champions. In 1962, second-placed Burnley had been denied entry to the Fairs Cup because it was based in a town, not a city. Nor did it host a large trade fair.

The Fairs Cup had a peculiar history. It had been conceived as a tournament between cities that were putting on trade fairs or huge business conventions. England was represented in the first Fairs Cup, which started in 1955, by a London team drawing players from Brentford, Chelsea, Fulham, Arsenal, Tottenham and West Ham. Only 12 teams entered but it took three years to complete.

The final in 1958 saw London and Barcelona draw 2-2 at Stamford Bridge, only for the Catalonians to win the return leg 6-0. The other cities to field select XIs were Copenhagen, Basle, Frankfurt, Zagreb, Staevnet, Leipzig, Vienna and Cologne, but the latter two had difficulties putting out teams and withdrew part the way through.

Another English city had a team in the first Fairs Cup but it was represented by the club that bears its name, Birmingham City. They had been Second Division Champions in 1955 so the modern-day criteria of finishing high in the top flight obviously did not apply. The city of Milan was represented by Inter.

Entry to the second Fairs Cup, in which 16 teams competed over the two seasons 1958-60, was again a matter of invitation. The two entrants from England were Chelsea and Birmingham who had finished 14th and 9th respectively in the First Division. Chelsea, champions in 1955, had wanted to compete in the first European Cup but English footballing chiefs had urged them not to take part, citing fears of fixture congestion. Entry to the next Fairs Cup may have been a consolatory gesture. All rounds were two-legged affairs and Birmingham did well, knocking out Cologne, Inter Milan and Belgrade before losing the final in 1960 to Barcelona. Chelsea went out at the second hurdle.

It raises the question of whether other English cities had been asked to take part in the Fifties. The city of Liverpool was still trying to deal with the heavy bomb damage from the Second World War and neither of the city's clubs impressed much in the Fifties. So it would not be surprising if Merseyside was overlooked. Credit to Birmingham City however for making the most of the opportunity that came their way. Strange as it may seem, they were one of English football's trailblazers in Europe.

Birmingham were the only English entrants in the third Fairs Cup, which was played in one season, 1960-61, and reached the final again, presumably much to the delight of young Jasper Carrott. They drew 2-2 with Roma in the first leg at St Andrews but lost the return in the Italian capital.

The 1961-62 Fairs Cup expanded to 28 teams and the three English entrants were newly Catterick-less Sheffield Wednesday, who had finished second in the league, Nottingham Forest, who were 14th, and Birmingham, 19th, who seemed to have automatic entry. Fifth-placed Everton may have declined a place because they had spent a big chunk of the summer of '61 playing in a tournament in North America.

The fifth Fairs Cup, 1962-63, was the first to take place without Birmingham City. Apparently the FA and the Football League both agreed that Burnley and Everton should be England's entrants. Ipswich, champions in 1962, had entered the European Cup while third-placed Tottenham had won the FA Cup and entered the Cup Winners Cup. But the Inter Cities Fairs Cup Committee turned down Burnley because it was not a city. The FA appealed on their behalf but without success. Burnley were puzzled that Dunfermline were allowed to compete. What might have helped the Scots' case was that the division between town and city was not as distinct in Scotland as in England. Also Dunfermline had once been Scotland's capital city.

What made the rejection of Burnley more bizarre was that they had played in the European Cup in 1960 after winning the League. Perhaps it did not help their case that the Burnley manager Harry Potts, who scored 16 goals in 63 games for Everton in the early 1950s, was so angry over refereeing decisions in the second leg at Reims that he ran onto the pitch to protest, only to be marched off by gendarmes and made to sit in the stand.

One can only wonder if a Fairs Cup bureaucrat once inquired about the location of the city of Everton. Certainly, somewhere along the way a rule was introduced that two or more clubs from the same city could not compete in the Fairs Cup in the same season. That rule was to significantly shorten the length of this book.

The second leg against Valerengen took place three weeks after the first leg. Number One in the singles charts now was another Fred Pickering lookalike, Roy Orbison, with Pretty Woman.

In the match programme the Evertonia column noted that it was our third successive season in Europe and we were still to get past the first hurdle. It added: "Although our games with Inter Milan last season aroused plenty of interest, the fact that we were knocked out so soon meant that Everton gained little in foreign recognition."

But confidence was high. Already aware that Kilmarnock would be our second round opponents, Evertonia wrote: "If we get through this next stage, we must have a good chance of winning the trophy."

He added: "Like any other international competition it has had its teething problems - particularly in so far as this country is concerned. Just which teams exactly from each country should take part in the competition was not very definitely stated. This resulted in mix-ups and hard feelings in some quarters. The position was smoothed out when the organisers made it clear that the Inter Cities Fairs Cup was primarily intended to be a money-spinning competition and that the intention was to restrict the participating clubs to those from big cities. It was not sufficient for a club to finish in a high place in its country's premier league, it must also be backed by a highly populated area - i.e., a major city. Things seem to be sorted out quite well now, however."

There were to be echoes of these sentiments more than 20 years later when Everton were among the prime movers in a project to set up a breakaway league for the biggest clubs.

The game saw the debut of a local lad who was to be a regular choice through the rest of the Sixties. It was one week before Tommy Wright's 20th birthday and he gave a solid display at right back. Later in his career he was to step onto the World Cup finals stage as part of an Everton squadette that, augmented by other First Division players, went close to winning the Jules Rimet trophy for England in Mexico.

One of the Valerengen players was also to make his mark in the World Cup finals, much later though, as a manager. Egil Olsen however was such a great dribbler that he went through life known as Drillo, after a Norwegian term for dribblng. But his ball skills were not confined to his feet. At one point in the second leg at Goodison, when play was interrupted while an injured player was treated, the 22-year-old delighted the crowd by juggling the ball with his head. Decades later he used his head to greater effect, coaching the Norway team to the finals of the 1994 and 1998 World Cup finals. It was a feat which made him a national hero.

But the man of the match that evening at Goodison was not Wright, nor Olsen; it was the goalkeeper Helge Sorlie - he was Hel to his mates. If it had not been for him, said Leslie Edwards of the Echo, the score would have ended 44-2 for Everton as he "put on the best exhibition of goalkeeping the ground has ever known".

His teammates battled manfully too; so much so that it nearly turned into a huge embarrassment for Everton because the Norwegians, with only nine fit players in the second half, were leading 2-1 after the first hour following goals by Ericsen and Olsen. Ericsen had a chance to put Valerengen 3-1 up and the tie almost level on aggregate, but by this time he was struggling with injury and the opportunity was missed. His striking partner Larsen was also unable to give his best, due to an injured shoulder. With substitutions not yet allowed, they just had to carry on.

It was a game in which Pickering's goal touch deserted him, partly due to Sorlie who stopped a string of goalbound shots and headers from Big Fred. Everton's salvation was Alex Young who not only gave a full display of his repertoire of flicked headers for which he was famed, but he also netted twice. The Norwegian Bjarne Hansen had the misfortune to score an own goal and Vernon made it 4-2 on the night; an aggregate of 9-4. Weh-heh, we were through to a second round.

4. KANGAROOS TO KILMARNOCK

Kilmarnock
Inter Cities Fairs Cup
1964-65

It wasn't like this in the brochure. European competition was meant to be about going to warmer climes. Yes, we did have that glamour game in Milan, but other than that we were always being sent to play in colder places - Dunfermline, Oslo, now Kilmarnock. There was probably only one person happy with the draw, Alex Parker, and the manager wouldn't let him go. Parker had been born and bred just seven miles from Kilmarnock in the town of Irvine. He had just lost his place in the team but was keen to travel up for the first leg. "I asked the manager if I could go up with the squad to watch the game, but he wouldn't let me. They just took the minimum in those days, the team and two or three reserves would be about it."

Some of his teammates may have been pleased about the short trip. The Blues had spent six weeks in the summer in Australia. The players had enjoyed the trip immensely but it was a long time to be away from their families. Brian Labone recalled: "We played at all the big cricket grounds: Perth, Adelaide, Melbourne, Brisbane,

Sydney. A lot of the top cricketers haven't done that. Harry Catterick could not come for some reason so Tommy Eggleston was in charge. Eggo told us if we won our games he wouldn't be too hard on the training."

Labone added: "It was one of the best trips I have ever been on. There was so many Scouse expats over there, it was like flying into Liverpool. I think we had £2 a day spending money but it was hard to spend it in a day because we were feted by all the expat Evertonians.

"The trip was sponsored by Craven A, a cigarette company, and their boss there put on some good do's for us. He had a big house by Sydney Harbour and he would put barbeques on for us. That's what started me smoking. He had these massive boxes of cigarettes there, a lot of the players smoked but Gordon West and I did not. We thought why should they get all these free cigarettes? Then we saw these cigarillos and we just got stuck into them. It's cost me thousands of pounds in cigars over the years. I've never smoked more than five cigarettes in 40 years, but plenty of cigars."

The Blues played five state sides and two games against an Australia XI. Labone said: "I remember in one game we went a goal down in five minutes and we remembered that training might become more severe. So we stepped up a gear and won that one. Then we went on a goal spree, winning games by five or six. We did have a few late nights out and towards the end the scores were getting closer and closer. If we had stayed another week, they would have beaten us."

The first game of the tour was on Saturday 2nd May at Sydney Cricket Ground where the home team, New South Wales, took a 7th minute lead, but Everton were 3-1 up at half-time and won 4-1. It was the first of seven wins in a gruelling schedule over 23 days which saw the Blues playing on Wednesdays and weekends.

Jimmy Gabriel scored five goals in a 8-1 win over Northern New South Wales in front of a 10,000 crowd in Newcastle. On Sunday 10th May at Olympic Park, Melbourne, the Blues faced the best footballers that Australia could muster, a national XI comprised of home-grown players and immigrants who included Austrian international centre forward Herbert Ninaus. More than 32,000 were present to see Ninaus score twice but Derek Temple also netted twice and Gabriel and Roy Vernon scored hat-tricks as Everton won 8-2. Next was a 415-mile trip to Adelaide where 20,000 saw the Blues beat South Australia 3-0.

Then a 725-mile journey to Sydney, the Showground, for another game against the Australia XI. A 40,000 crowd saw Ninaus score again but Everton won 5-1 with two goals from Johnny Morrissey and one apiece from Gabriel, Alex Scott and Colin Harvey. Seat-belts were fastened again as the Blues flew 2,000 miles to the other side of the country for a game in front of 20,000 at Perth, in which Western Australia were beaten 14-1. Derek Temple scored five and there were hat-tricks for Scott, Vernon and Ulsterman Jimmy Hill. Then there was a 1,700-mile flight for the final game on Sunday 24th May at Olympic Park, Melbourne, in which 29,000 saw Everton beat Victoria 3-1 with one goal by Temple and two from Vernon.

It was a record of played seven, won seven, scored 45, conceded 7. The team had flown more than 10,000 miles to Sydney, then travelled around 5,000 miles criss-crossing Australia before making the long flight back home. Given their exertions in the summer, it would not have been surprising if the Blues were beginning to flag a little when they travelled to Kilmarnock for the first leg on 11th November, 1964. Notably, since knocking out Valerengen, the Blues had drawn one and lost three league games.

Kilmarnock would be no pushover. The early to mid-Sixties was probably the era when Scottish club football was at its most competitive. This was the one period when Rangers and Celtic faced sustained competition to their supremacy from at least one other club. Between 1905 and 1947, the title was always won by one of the Glasgow giants. But between 1960 and 1965, Hearts, Dundee and Kilmarnock all won the title and were contenders in other seasons.

Certainly, 1964-65 was to be the greatest season ever in Kilmarnock's history, and not just because they played at Goodison. 'Killie' were to win the Scottish championship for the first time in their long history and in a manner that could have been scripted by a film-maker. The star was not a player, but the manager. Willie Waddell is still heralded as one of Glasgow Rangers' greatest players. An outstanding winger, viewed by the Ibrox faithful as a superman, he was capped 17 times for Scotland between 1947 and 1955 before moving into journalism. This footballing Clark Kent was lured into management by Kilmarnock in 1957.

"Killie" had only ever won the Division 2 championship - twice in Victorian days - and the Scottish Cup, twice in the 1920s. Waddell however was to put them among the big boys. He introduced full-time contracts for players and Killie soon became championship contenders, finishing runners-up in 1960, 1961, 1963 and 1964. They also reached the final of the League Cup twice and the Scottish Cup. A trophy eluded them, but it was soon to come.

The drama began a few weeks before the Everton game. It was following a 5-2 win over Celtic that Waddell announced he was leaving the club at the end of the season to return to journalism. The supporters were devastated. They had just enjoyed a fantastic night of European football. In the first round of the Fairs Cup, Kilmarnock had travelled to Eintracht Frankfurt for the first leg and lost 3-0. In the second minute of the second leg, Eintracht scored again, but Kilmarnock then scored five to win on aggregate 5-4. All this would have given Catterick plenty of food for thought, especially as Killie were on a run of 26 home games unbeaten and top of the league.

When Everton travelled up to Scotland for the first leg, they were trying to halt an alarming slump in form. Since the Valerengen game, the Blues had drawn at Blackpool then lost to Blackburn, Arsenal and Leeds. The 3-1 defeat at Highbury was to be the last of 219 games that Parker played for Everton. When Leeds won 1-0 at Goodison, the No.2 shirt was worn by youngster Barrie Rees. It was shortly to become the property of Tommy Wright, who had made his debut against the Norwegians. But for the game at Kilmarnock, Catterick chose to switch Dennis Stevens to right back. The team was: Rankin, Stevens, Brown, Gabriel, Labone, Harris, Temple, Young, Pickering, Vernon, Morrissey.

There had been 15,000 in the ground to see Kilmarnock's sensational win in the previous round over Eintracht Frankfurt. The visit of Everton brought in a crowd of more than 23,000. But the performance of Kilmarnock never hit the heights of the display against the Germans. Being an Anglo-Scots encounter, there was a fair amount of tension and some crisp tackling but none of the nastiness that marred the first leg between Everton and Dunfermline. Gabriel was effervescent in midfield while Alex Young played deeper than usual as Catterick tried to shackle the home side. Everton were pinned back for periods of the first half but at the interval it was still 0-0.

However within 15 minutes of the restart, Everton were two up. Temple put in a shot to which the keeper Campbell Forsyth got a hand but could only deflect it into the net. Then a few minutes later Morrissey scored a superb solo goal, beating two men then hitting a powerful shot that gave the keeper no chance. Years later this was to become a trademark of his son John who rose through the youth teams at Everton before enjoying a successful career at Tranmere.

It was Kilmarnock's first season in Europe but they had gained considerable experience of foreign opposition, having spent three summers in North America competing in the International Soccer League. Among their opponents had been Everton.

The ISL was set up in 1960, by Bill Cox, a former owner of the Philadelphia Phillies baseball club. He believed that the first-generation immigrant communities, notably from Europe, could kickstart a major football league in North America. The ISL was to be the catalyst. Each summer for several years he imported leading clubs from Europe who would play each other and specially-assembled American teams.

Everton competed in the second year of the ISL, in 1961, playing nine games. The tournament was divided into two sections with the winners of each meeting in a two-legged final. Everton dominated Section 1, played in May and June, beating Kilmarnock, Karlsruhe of West Germany, Dinamo Bucharest, the Turkish team Besiktas, New York Americans and Montreal Concordia. The Blues' only defeat in Section 1 was to the Brazilian team Bangu, who had won the 1960 tournament, beating Kilmarnock in the final.

Section 2, whose games were played in July, contained Dukla Prague, Monaco, Red Star Belgrade, Espanyol, Rapid Vienna, Shamrock Rovers, Montreal Concordia again and the Israeli team Petah Tikva. Dukla won all their games except the one against Montreal which they drew.

Everton had travelled back to England while Section 2 took place. They then flew back to America for a two-legged final against Dukla Prague. Even jet lag would not account for a 7-2 defeat in the first game. The Prague team won the next leg 2-0 for a 9-2 aggregate to take home to Communist Czechoslovakia the Dwight D. Eisenhower Trophy.

Kilmarnock had reached the 1960 final after defeating Bayern Munich, the Irish club Glenavon, Burnley, New York Americans and drawing against Nice. Killie had returned to the ISL, not only in 1961 but also 1963. They were to go again at the end of this season.

Kilmarnock travelled to Merseyside for the second leg still hoping they could pull off another shock turnaround. Vernon, Ray Wilson and Tony Kay were ruled out. The team was: Rankin, Harris, Brown, Gabriel, Labone, Stevens, Temple, Young, Pickering, Harvey, Morrissey.

There was a surprise for the 30,000 crowd when Everton strode out in white shirts and black shorts. It seemed there had been a mix-up, if not a row, over kit colours and Killie had insisted on playing in their traditional blue and white stripes. In addition, Stevens was wearing the No.6 shirt, but again played right-back while Brian Harris was left-half.

Kilmarnock were without their captain Frank Beattie but still they began the game as if they believed they could wipe out Everton's two-goal lead. Killie got off to a great start, taking the lead through Brian McIlroy to reduce Everton's aggregate lead to just one goal. It looked as though they were level when a fine effort from Ronnie Hamilton seemed goalbound until Andy Rankin brought off a great save.

Harris, playing left-back, had suffered a cut to his head early in the game but played on. Young was in vintage form, Morrissey was having another good game and Colin Harvey was a joy to watch in midfield. Stevens was giving a sterling performance at right-back.

Harvey scored for Everton to make it 1-1 on the night and 3-1 on aggregate to Everton. Still the Scottish side battled away but after Fred Pickering latched on to a through ball and drove it past the keeper to put Everton 4-1 up on aggregate, the Killie resolve seemed to ebb away.

Young scored with a shot that might have been meant as a cross. Then Forsyth was judged to have handballed just outside the penalty area. Young prodded the ball, Sandy Brown ran over it and Pickering crashed a shot into the back of the net to make it 4-1 on the night and 6-1 on aggregate.

Kilmarnock were out of the Fairs Cup but that season they went on to win the Scottish championship in a remarkable game on the last day of the season. They travelled to Hearts who were two points ahead at the top of the table. Due to the complexities of the old-fashioned system of goal average, Kilmarnock had to win by two clear goals. If Hearts lost, but scored in a defeat, the "Jam tarts" would win the title. Kilmarnock were 2-0 up at half time, then had to hang on through a nail-biting second half to win the championship by 0.042 of a goal.

Waddell, as he had said, returned to newspapers. In 1969, after a four-year spell in journalism, Waddell became manager of Rangers, later becoming general manager and was largely influential in the reconstruction of Ibrox after the disaster in 1971 when 66 fans were killed on a stairway at the end of an Old Firm match. He became a director at Rangers before dying from a heart attack in 1992, aged 71.

5. BACK TO HIS ROOTS

Manchester United
Inter Cities Fairs Cup
1964 - 65

Everton chairman John Moores was going back to his roots. Born and bred in Manchester, he had set up the Littlewood Football Pool in 1923 and, with schoolboy helpers, given out the company's first 4,000 coupons outside Old Trafford before a United home match. The punters were unimpressed. Only 35 coupons were filled in and posted to the office that 27-year-old Moores had just set up in Liverpool.

But within five years it was thriving. In 1932 he diversified, setting up a company in which people paid in regular amounts of money before ordering goods that were despatched through the post. Littlewoods Mail Order was born. Five years later he opened the first Littlewoods shop in Blackpool. By 1940 there was a chain of 24 stores dotted around the country. After the war, John and his brother Cecil continued to oversee the Littlewoods empire which had three arms: football pools, mail order and high street stores.

In January 1956, he celebrated his 60th birthday, a notable milestone in anyone's life, and perhaps he thought it time to try and make an impact outside the world of business. It is generally accepted that he already held shares in both Everton and Liverpool. In the 1950s, it was common practice for many Merseysiders to attend both teams' home games. Moores' acquisition of shares in both clubs can perhaps be seen as a businessman's extension of this bi-partisan approach. Moores was also a golfing companion of the Liverpool chairman Tom Williams.

But his first, lasting, high-profile step outside Littlewoods was into the art world. An amateur artist, Moores was an admirer of Liverpool's Walker Art Gallery and its fine collection of paintings. But he felt there was a London bias in the arts world. So he suggested that the Walker mount an exhibition embracing "the best and most vital" contemporary paintings. He would put forward the prize money to attract the best young artists. It was intended as a one-off, but became a regular event, held every two years. By 1965, the John Moores Exhibition was regarded as one of Britain's leading arts events. It still runs today with the 24th staged in autumn 2006 as part of the Liverpool Biennial festival.

A move into active involvement in a football club required more planning because one of his three businesses was based on encouraging Britons to try and forecast which games would end in draws. He had to tread carefully. So, before he became a director of Everton in March 1960, he relinquished his association with the pools arm of Littlewoods, leaving it in the control of his brother Cecil.

So, 42 years after standing outside Old Trafford getting strange looks as he handed out coupons, Moores could return as a king. It was the first time two English clubs had been drawn against each other in the Fairs Cup and it was one of the first "Battles of Britain" in European competition - plus, for the Everton supporters, it was another exotic European destination.

The two clubs, both formed in 1878, had very similar records. Everton had been English champions six times and FA Cup winners twice. United had won the title five times and the FA Cup thrice. That's 8-8. The two had met in the 1963 Charity Shield with the Blues winning 4-0, giving the Evertonians of January 1965 a slight edge in bragging rights.

Like Everton, United had travelled to Scandinavia for the first leg of their first round match in September 1964. They drew 1-1 in Sweden with Djurgaardens IF before hammering them 6-1 at Old Trafford. But that was nothing compared to the next round. United faced Borussia Dortmund who the previous season had been European Cup semi-finalists. United went to West Germany and won 6-1 with hat-tricks from George Best and Bobby Charlton. At Old Trafford, United won 4-0 for a 10-1 aggregate. "We were unfortunate to draw Everton, a powerful side that had won the League in 1963, in the next round," says Denis Law's autobiography, The King.

Strangely, the 1960s was the first time that both clubs had enjoyed illustrious spells in the same era. In the inter-war years, Everton lifted the title three times and the FA Cup once. In contrast, United won nothing; they were also-rans. But when Everton were struggling during the Fifties, United were one of the best teams in the land, winning the title three times.

In January 1965 Matt Busby was in his 20th season as manager, having just assembled his third great Manchester United team. His life is one of football's epic stories. The Scot had played for Manchester City from 1929 to 1936 when he was sold to Liverpool for £8,000, spending three years at Anfield where he became captain. When the war came to an end, Busby was about to become coach at Liverpool. But in June 1945, at the age of 36, he was offered the job of manager at Manchester United. He could either be a No.2 or a No.1 - he chose the latter.

It was a daunting task that faced him. Not only had United not won a trophy since 1911, but also Old Trafford had been bombed to bits and would not reopen for another three years. They were Salford's finest, but hardly a glamour club.

The cornerstone of Busby's first great team was Johnny Carey whom he made captain. The future Everton manager lifted United's first trophy in 37 years when they won the FA Cup in 1948. Goodison Park had played a part. In the fourth round, United were drawn at home to play Liverpool. Due to the bomb damage at Old Trafford, United ground-shared with Manchester City but on this day Maine Road was unavailable. Around 74,000 crammed into Goodison to see Busby's team beat his old club 3-0.

Credited with playing fine football, United were league runners-up in four of the first five seasons after the war before finally winning the title in 1952. Such was the influence of the cultured Carey that he was named Footballer of the Year in 1949 and selected to captain the Rest of Europe against Great Britain. Busby offered Carey a coaching job at Old Trafford but the Irishman was offered the manager's job at Blackburn where he was in charge for five years before taking over at Goodison.

Busby's second great team won the title in 1956 and 1957 when they came close to the Double, only losing the FA Cup final 2-1 to Aston Villa in a final famed for a controversial goal when Peter McParland barged United keeper Ray Woods over the line. What made this United team all the more remarkable was that Busby did not buy a player from 1953 to 1957. Some had been bought years ago but many had come through the youth ranks. Hence the term, the Busby Babes.

This raises the question: If Busby had remained at Liverpool, would they instead have had the run of success in the Fifties that United enjoyed? For after winning the first post-war championship in 1947, Liverpool fell away, becoming a mid-table team before being relegated in 1954 to the Second Division where they spent eight seasons.

Busby was a pioneer of European football. The Football League had a Little England mentality and frowned at its teams playing in Europe, citing concerns over the ability to fulfil fixtures. Chelsea, champions in 1955, were bullied out of competing in the first European Cup. The same heavy moves were made against United but Busby persuaded his board to stand firm. The United chairman was a former Everton player, Harold Hardman, who had played in our 1906 FA Cup winning team.

United became the first English team to enter the European Cup, reaching the semi-finals in March 1957. Having retained the championship, they entered the European Cup again but the venture ended in tragedy. In February 1958, following a quarter-final in Yugoslavia against Red Star Belgrade, their plane stopped for refuelling in Germany. On its third attempt to take off from Munich, the plane crashed, killing 23 passengers, including eight players aged in their Twenties.

Busby spent weeks in hospital. After the trauma of Munich, the best that United could do was to carry on playing and stay in the First Division. United finished the 1957-58 season in ninth place while Wolves won the title. It is noteworthy that UEFA invited not only Wolves, but also United to take part in the next season's European Cup. Following pressure from the Football League, United declined.

Busby gave notice that he had assembled a third great team in the 1963 FA Cup Final when United outplayed Leicester. But Everton were too good for them in the Charity Shield a few months later. However United were then given a gift from the gods - George Best. Aged only 18 on the night of our Fairs Cup tie, the baby-faced Belfast boy with the Beatle haircut was on his way to being one of the most famed footballers of all time. Perhaps fitting then that Number One in the charts was Georgie Fame and the Blue Flames with the energetic number Yeh, Yeh, which could have doubled as the soundtrack for one of his marvellous, mazy runs.

Present at Old Trafford to watch the first leg on Wednesday 20th January, 1965, was England manager Alf Ramsey. He had vowed that England would win the World Cup to be held in England the following year. Very much in his thoughts was Fred Pickering who was in a rich vein of form, having scored in seven of his last eight matches in which Everton had been unbeaten. Ramsey had already picked Pickering three times for England and Big Fred had scored in each game, starting with a hat-trick against the United States in a 10-0 win in New York. His other goals came against Northern Ireland and Belgium.

Catterick was facing several dilemmas. Would the young Tommy Wright cope with the occasion or would nerves get the better of him? After all, Catterick did have the option of calling on the experience of Sandy Brown. Another dilemma was over Colin Harvey and Dennis Stevens who were not fully fit. One could tell how highly Catterick rated Stevens by the fact that the versatile right-sided player had missed the previous eight games but the manager decided to play him at Old Trafford. Catterick also showed his faith in Harvey, selecting him too.

Everton had just the start they wanted, taking an early lead. It was in the 13th minute when Tommy Wright put a ball through the middle for Pickering to chase in competition with his marker Bill Foulkes. The United centre-half tried to clear but he was under pressure from Big Fred and the ball fell kindly for Pickering who raced towards goal. Foulkes recovered well and put in another challenge but Pickering held him off and, as goalkeeper Pat Dunne came out, slotted the ball into the corner. It was a birthday goal for Big Fred who had turned 24 the day before the game.

Also in fine form were Gordon West and Brian Labone as Everton battled to hold out Best, Law and Charlton. In the first 30 minutes West made four brilliant saves from Charlton. Labone was marking the United centre-forward David Herd out of the game. But on 33 minutes Jimmy Gabriel played a slack back-pass which was pounced upon by John Connelly who beat West to equalise.

Fortunately Best was being well shackled by Wright and the Belfast boy only really threatened when switching to the right wing in the second half. "He never did much against us because Tommy Wright used to play him brilliantly," said Labone. "Tom was very quick and Best could not turn on the magic. You could never totally blot George out because he was so good, but Tommy would take care of him very well."

It looked as if United were about to take the lead early in the second half when a header from Law seemed goalbound until West produced a breathtaking save - one of several he pulled off in the game. The game ended 1-1, setting up another enthralling encounter in the second leg in three weeks' time.

But before then there was a FA Cup fourth round tie against Don Revie's Leeds United. By now, the Moody Blues were Number One in the singles charts, with Go Now - the title was perhaps an omen for the Blues. We drew 1-1 at Elland Road, with Pickering on the scoresheet again. Three days later, on Tuesday 2nd February, we lost the replay at Goodison in front of 66,000. On the following Saturday there was the relatively small matter of a league match at Goodison against Birmingham, then on Tuesday 9th February the second leg against United, our third game at Goodison in eight days.

The reader might have wondered why Moores decided to base Littlewoods in Liverpool in 1923, rather than his home city of Manchester? The answer perhaps lies in the love of a good woman. In that same year he married Ruby Knowles, daughter of a Liverpool shipping clerk. Apparently he had lodged with her family while working on Merseyside.

The decision may also have had something to do with issues of security in the early stages of the pools operation. He had to guard against the possibility of fraud by employees. Did he think it would be better if the staff that did the checking of coupons were a good distance away from the staff who had bundles of coupons to hand out? Whatever the reason for the location, it had huge repercussions because Littlewods became one of the biggest employers in Merseyside for decades. Ultimately, it had a big impact too on Everton football club.

John Moores and his brother Cecil settled in Formby, a pleasant suburb of Liverpool; not that Formby impressed everybody. Cecil's granddaughter Louise was 29 when she was interviewed by journalist Deborah Ross for a feature in the Daily Mail in December 1993. In the article Louise - who would have been a baby when Everton played United in the Fairs Cup - gives a rare insight into the world of the Moores in the Sixties.

Louise's childhood was extraordinary. Not because it was snazzy or flash but because it wasn't. She grew up in Victoria Road in Formby, a distinctly unglamorous district of Liverpool. The Moores all lived in the same street. Sir John - known as Mr John by everyone who worked for him - lived at one end. Cecil lived at the other. The houses in between spilled with uncles, aunts and cousins.

The houses were nothing special. "Ours was a Twenties', two-storey, pebble-dash house. Very ordinary. Neither my grandfather or Sir John believed in frills and they abhorred social climbers. If someone bought a massive house, they would laugh at them. They'd say 'What do you want such a big house for?' They never forgot their roots. They remained working class to the end. And if we ever got snotty, we were quickly brought back to earth."

A recurring theme of descriptions of Sir John is that he was very careful with his money, even though he had so much of it. Although fabulously wealthy, he did not want to buy a big house. He wanted to help Everton, but why give money to the club when he could help the Blues just by making interest-free loans and lending the club his business expertise.

The Everton programme for the return leg against United cost "a tanner", that's six old pence, or two and a half pence of today's money. The next away game was at West Ham on Saturday 13th and Sunniways Coachways were advertising their trips to East London which left on Friday night at 11.30pm. The fare was 37 shillings and 9 pence, around £1.89p.

United came to Goodison on the day that The Righteous Brothers went to Number One with You've Lost That Lovin' Feeling. It's not something that could be said of the programme editor who, noting that Cologne were playing at Anfield the following night, told readers: "We want to wish Liverpool all success tomorrow, and may they become the first British club to win the European Cup. Let's get it on Merseyside. That's our primary wish." Hhmmm.

United started the game flying, playing with a panache and a passion that could only be admired. They took the lead in the sixth minute. Connelly picked the ball up on the halfway line and ran at the Everton defence then played a glorious one-two with Law before shooting home. The United fans danced in delight; the Evertonians just looked at each other.

Busby's men had several opportunities to stretch their lead. Everton however continued to work at their game and began to push United on to the backfoot. Harvey fired into the side netting,

Gabriel blasted over, Pickering went on a great run before sending in a shot that Dunne turned away for a corner. Vernon showed his verve and guile while Scott and Temple wasted opportunities. A Pickering free-kick was turned on to the post by Dunne. Everton had Goodison roaring in support. Finally the breakthrough came. Nobby Stiles needlessly gave away a free kick, obstructing Vernon when there seemed to be little danger. It was indirect and Stevens gave the impression he was going to take it but ran over the ball. Pickering stepped forward and crashed a shot that ended in the back of the net. It had taken a deflection, but the Evertonians didn't care. It was 1-1 on the night and 2-2 on aggregate.

It was then all Everton, or so it seemed to the Blues in the crowd. Temple, Stevens and Harvey all had chances but United continued to hold out although it seemed only a matter of time before the Blues scored again. Pickering brought another save out of Dunne while Vernon hit the upright. If Everton needed a warning about their wastefulness in front of goal, it came when Best went on an electrifying run that nearly resulted in a wonder goal. But it was with 15 minutes left that United carried out a smash and grab raid. Law had had a quiet game but played a neat pass into the path of Connelly. The winger hit a shot that West parried. The ball rolled sidewards in the most kindly manner possible for Herd who smashed it into the Everton net. "I remember David Herd scoring, that was at the Park End," said Labone. "I don't know where I was."

Out of the FA Cup and the Fairs Cup in the space of a week. We'd lost that winnin' feeling. Had our finishing let us down? Or was it more to do with United having so many matchwinners in their team? Law saw it as a tale of two goalkeepers, with one having a little more luck. He remarked in his book how United had been held in the first leg "thanks to a sparkling display from Everton's England goalkeeper Gordon West". He said Everton had been favourites for the second leg but Dunne was their hero, "with several top-class saves including one which rolled along the goalline, hit the post and bounced back into his arms". The path of that ball was yet another example of the thin line between success and failure. Der ball ist rund.

In the FA Cup Leeds went on to Wembley, losing 2-1 as Liverpool won the FA Cup final for the first time in their history. Manchester United overcame Racing Strasbourg in the next round of the Fairs Cup but lost to Ferencvaros in a semi-final that went to a third game. United however won the championship, pipping Leeds on goal difference.

Busby retired as United manager in April 1969. During his 24 years in charge United had won five league championships, two FA Cups and the 1968 European Cup. His final championship success in 1967 was to be United's last for 26 years.

In 1965, Everton finished fourth in the title race, five points ahead of Liverpool. Another 40 years were to pass before we would finish ahead of Liverpool without us winning the league. Put another way: Apart from when we won the title in 1970, 1985 and 1987, we consistently finished below our neighbours over the following four decades. And yet so many of us have maintained over the years that we were always better than them. Of course we were. It's just that only us could see it.

6. GIVING HITLER THE BLUES

Nuremburg
Inter Cities Fairs Cup
1965-66

Everton were drawn to play the most famous club in Bavaria and the most successful in the history of German football. In 1965 Nuremburg had won the German championship more times, eight, than any other club. In contrast, their Bavarian rivals Bayern Munich only had one championship to their name and that was back in the 1930s. So it was unfortunate that after the first leg between Nuremburg and Everton, Harry Catterick felt compelled to describe the Germans as "the dirtiest side I have ever seen".

Given the great respect for German football teams in recent decades, it is surprising to learn that there was no nationwide league until 1963. This was nothing to do with the political divide between West and East following the Second World War. There was not even a league covering the whole of West Germany until the Bundesliga kicked off in 1963.

Until then, clubs had played in regional leagues and the winners of each Oberligen went into play-offs which resulted in a championship final. Some of these were phenomenal. VFB Leipzig and Sp Vgg Furth, who were Nuremburg's local rivals, were level after 90 minutes in the 1914 final then played another 63 minutes before Furth scored a winner. It was an early case of the "Golden Goal" rule.

But this was nothing compared to the 1922 final when Nuremburg and Hamburg played for three hours, 10 minutes before the referee called a halt due to darkness. The replay was another sensation. Nuremburg had one player sent off for kicking an opponent in the stomach, a second was taken off injured, another was sent off and one collapsed. Having just seven players on the pitch broke the rules and the game was stopped with the score at 2-2. The record books state that there was no title winner that year. Even so, Nuremburg still won the German championship five times in the 1920s. Such was their dominance that they were known in Bavaria simply as The Club.

They won the title again in 1936. But, sadly, by this time Nuremburg was better known for Nazism. The city had a rich medieval history and a reputation as the centre of the German Renaissance. Consequently Adolf Hitler decided in 1933, the year he came to power, that it would be the most appropriate place to host the annual convention of his National Socialist Party. Each September 500,000 Nazis would flock to Nuremburg for a week of parades and propaganda. It was there in September 1935 that the Nazi Congress passed laws which basically stripped Jewish people of their civil liberties and rights; subsequently these became known as "the Nuremburg Laws". It was due to the high profile of the city in the Third Reich that it was to later host the War Crimes Trials, further linking the city with Nazism.

Apparently Hitler had very little interest in football, but being a ultra-nationalist, he wanted the nation's sports teams to do well, especially at the 1936 Olympic Games which were to be held in Berlin. Bizarrely, Everton played a key part in the pre-tournament preparations of the German football squad. We played no less than five games against them.

Shortly after our final league game of the 1935-36 season, a 5-0 win over Preston on Saturday 2nd May, an Everton party was sailing to Hamburg aboard the cruise liner New York which had stopped in England on its way from America. On Saturday 9th May, Everton played a German XI in Hamburg, winning 3-0. The team moved on to Duisberg where the following Wednesday they lost 4-1 in front of a crowd of 20,000. The next weekend it was a 3-1 win in Frankfurt. Then on Friday 22nd May, the Daily Post reported: "Berlin, Thursday - About 25,000 spectators saw a German national side defeat Everton by 4 goals to 2 at the Adolf Hitler Stadium this evening. Everton set the pace at the start, but although attacking hotly were unable to pierce the strong defence."

The Everton party was accompanied on its travels by Otto Nerz who in 1926 had been appointed the first coach of the German national football team. "He had a clean-cut, stern face, wore his hair extremely short and watched the world suspiciously through steel-rimmed glasses," wrote Ulrich Hesse-Lichtenberger in his fascinating book, Tor! The Story of German Football. "He never smiled, had no time for niceties and valued discipline, conditioning and strategy."

Everton secretary Theo Kelly, who was sending reports to the local press from Germany, saw him in a different light. "Otto Nerz has been the life and soul of the officials group, and when we were consoling each other after the second game that the goals against did not exceed the aggregate of goals for, he chipped in to say that he 'would make arrangements to keep down the rate of exchange'! One of his wise-isms is repeatedly borne out in fact, viz, 'With the best we are satisfied.' His ju-jitsu tricks have been freely applied, much to the discomfiture of those nearest to him."

Writing from Germany after the last game of the three-week tour, a draw in Nuremburg, Kelly commented on the tally of won two, lost two, drawn one, with Everton scoring 10 and conceding 10. "To finish all square against Germany's best is a feat of no mean value. Consider that the Germans were playing for their place in the national team at Olympia and you will see that the matches were test matches of the sternest kind. Every player who will be chosen to represent Germany in the Olympic Games at Berlin in August has played against our team on this tour."

Or, as Joe Mercer put it more succinctly, Everton had fulfilled the role of "trial horses". The club was probably flattered to be asked to provide the opposition for a national team preparing for a major event. But I find it discomforting to think that the club had agreed to play the national team of Nazi Germany. There was considerable concern in Britain at this time over Hitler's aggressive policies at home and abroad. After taking power in 1933, many of the brave Germans who openly opposed him were arrested and, if not shot, placed in Dachau concentration camp which had opened in that same year. Jewish people were being forced out of sports clubs. Internationally, Germany had withdrawn from the League of Nations in 1933. Just a couple of months before our 1936 tour, German troops had marched into the demilitarised Rhineland zone, contravening the Versailles and Locarno treaties signed after the First World War.

There is of course the argument that sports teams should not get involved in politics and that games such as football can be useful in bringing people together. And I did not live in 1936 when many people were dearly hoping, possibly even assuming, that Britain would not be plunged so soon into another massive war. It is interesting to note that two years later the Football Association sent an England team to Berlin to play Germany in a friendly even though Hitler had taken over Austria. Before kick-off the England players gave the Nazi salute in front of a crowd of 110,000 that included Göring, Goebbels and Hess.

I would assume that if the Everton board had known the full scale of horrors the Nazi regime was to unleash a few years later, they would never have gone.

Noticeably, one absentee from the 1936 tour was Dixie Dean. He had missed the last game of the season and might have been injured. But his first biographer Nick Walsh, who wrote his book in the 1970s after a series of interviews with Dean, tells of an earlier Everton tour of Germany which included a game against Dresden, apparently attended by Goring and other Nazis. "Dean as captain, and holding a personal abhorrence of the Nazi system, was anxious to achieve a convincing victory," wrote Walsh. At the toss-up, he had a disagreement with the opposing captain over whether to use a size 5 or size 4 football. "As neither captain nor referee could speak the other's language Dean quickly pointed to the centre stand picking up the size 4 ball as he walked over." The German captain and referee thought Dean wanted the dignitaries to resolve the row and followed him. "Arriving in front of the stand Dean held up the size 4 ball displaying it before the VIPs. He then bounced it and promptly kicked it high over the stand and out of sight." They used the size 5 ball and Dean scored a hat trick.

Walsh also tells of an incident in Cologne where Jimmy Dunn was robbed and chased the thief who managed to get away. Dunn was arrested for causing a commotion. Dean subsequently went to the police station, a row ensued, two policemen pulled out their truncheons and the Everton centre-forward woke up in a cell with lumps on his head and two broken fingers. He was taken to court and fined. Quite possibly, Dean simply refused to go on the 1936 tour.

So, what happened to the German football team in the 1936 Olympics? After beating Luxembourg 9-0 in the first round, they were drawn to play Norway on 7th August. The Olympics offered Hitler an element of credibility and the prospect of a huge propaganda boost if the Third Reich's sportsmen did well. A top aide advised the Fuhrer to go and watch the football team on the basis that they "will win gold". He turned up for the Norway game, accompanied by Goebbels, Goring and Hess. Germany were expected to win comfortably and did dominate the game but Norway took an early lead and clung on to it before scoring a second in the 85th minute, at which point the Fuhrer stormed out. As one might expect, Nerz the manager came in for heavy criticism, with a lack of match practice being cited. The only team they had played in the period prior to the tournament, said Hesse-Lichtenberger in his book, was Everton. Had we somehow put the mockers on Nazi gold? I'd like to think so.

After the outbreak of the Second World War, the German championship continued until 1944 even though clubs were badly hit by the loss of players to the military and by fuel shortages which hindered travel. Schalke won the title in 1940 and 1942, to draw level with Nuremburg on the number of titles claimed, six each. But the first champions after the resumption were Nuremburg, beating Kaiserslautern in the final, taking their haul of titles to seven. This would have provided some cheer to a devastated city. Allied bombing raids had left 90 per cent of its Old Town reduced to rubble. The only German city left in a worse state was Dresden.

Nerz had stepped down from his post shortly after the Olympics and was succeeded by his assistant, Sepp Herberger, who remained in charge of the national team until 1964. Consequently he is seen by many as the father figure of German football.

Herberger was a great believer in the unpredictability of the game. He coined the phrase "Der ball ist rund" (The ball is round) by which he meant: That's the only thing that's for sure, anything can happen during a match. It's a gloriously simple philosophy that not only offers encouragement to any team facing opponents deemed stronger, but also makes a mockery of anyone pessimistically dwelling too long on a run of defeats. It also highlights how a game can be settled by a piece of good fortune, or vice vera. I thought this very apt for a book on Everton.

But having always abhorred Hitler and having visited Auschwitz in summer 2005, I have wondered if it was right to use so prominently a phrase coined by a man who coached the German national team when Hitler was in power.

I read again the book Tor!, in which Hesse-Lichtenberger portrays Herberger as a basically decent man so obsessed with football he compiled in his lifetime 361 thick files of notes on games and players, adding: "We know that he once came to the help of a Jew who was being attacked on the street and that he always stuck by his family doctor, who was married to a Jew and ostracised by almost everybody else."

After the war, Germans who had held positions of seniority were assessed as to whether they had been committed to the Nazi cause. Herberger had joined the National Socialist Party in 1933, "guided by Nerz and Linnemann (head of the German FA) who had told him it would further his career, but the occupying forces correctly did not judge him to be a committed Nazi, which spared Herberger the internment camp," said Hesse-Lichtenberger. But that was the fate that befell Nerz who "would practically starve in Soviet captivity and passed away from meningitis in Sachsenhausen in 1949," wrote Hesse-Lichtenberger.

This question over Herberger touches on a range of issues, most notably the relationship between the individual and the state, especially a totalitarian one. I came to the conclusion, albeit a simplistic one, that if Herberger had been leader of Germany, the only people with anything to worry about would have been those who hated football because there would have been so much of it, and then the objectors would have been allowed to get on with their lives. In any case, and perhaps most importantly, the phrase - Der ball ist rund - is purely a footballing term.

Never was the phrase borne out more than in the 1954 World Cup finals in Switzerland. Hot favourites were Hungary who had chalked up 30 wins in an unbeaten run stretching back three years. Herberger's West Germany team did well just to qualify for the tournament. The amateur ethos was still widespread in the country and even the top players had jobs outside football. Team captain Fritz Walter ran a laundry, while goalscoring hero Helmut Rahn was a truck driver.

In the group stages Hungary had run up a 8-3 scoreline over West Germany who then surprised everyone by making it to the final where they faced again the Mighty Magyars. Another rout looked likely when Hungary went 2-0 up in the first eight minutes but Nuremburg striker Max Morlock pulled one back a couple of minutes later. Rahn equalised before half-time. The second half was a tense affair. With just six minutes left, a loose ball fell to Rahn who put the Germans 3-2 up.

This triumph on a football pitch, the Miracle of Berne, is seen as having given the German nation - shattered by the war, humiliated by defeat and ridden with guilt over the horrors inflicted in its name by the Nazi regime - a renewed sense of self-belief.

But it also hampered the efforts of those in West Germany who wanted a national league. The regional structure of the championship had continued after the war. It would have been like Everton playing only a dozen or so North West clubs, hoping that they would qualify to play the winners of the North East, Midlands and London zones in the national championship play-offs. Critics said the structure of the game in Germany restricted the development of the best players, the top clubs and the national team. They pointed out that the Oberligens did not have enough strong teams to really test the local giants, such as Nuremburg, who would stroll through some of their regional league games. Similarly, their best players had few opportunities to play against high quality opposition. Herberger frequently argued: "If we want to remain competitive internationally we have to raise our expectations at the national level."

But when it came to setting up a national West German league, Herberger and his allies also had to contend with the often-parochial regional football associations who wished to retain their power. There were also rows about which teams should be included, plus differences over a licensing system that was devised for the clubs. However, after West Germany performed poorly in the 1962 World Cup finals in Chile, agreement was reached and the Bundesliga finally kicked off in August 1963, with Nuremburg among the 16 teams.

When Nuremburg faced Everton they had a Hungarian coach, Jeno Czaknady, who was in his first season, and a technical director, Riemke, who had travelled to Merseyside the previous weekend to see the derby at Anfield. Nuremburg had had no game the previous weekend due to West Germany playing Sweden in a World Cup qualifier. The Nuremburg team of 1965 had three German internationals: centre half Ferdinand Wenauer, left half Stefan Reisch and centre forward Heinz Strehl. Curiously, however, the author could find no evidence of any Nuremburg players in the West German squad that played in the World Cup finals in England at the end of the season.

The trip to Nuremburg was not a new experience for two of the Everton team. Just a few months earlier, Derek Temple had made his England debut there in a 1-0 win over West Germany. Ray Wilson was also in the squad that day in May but did not make the team.

Catterick had turned for advice to Matt Busby who had seen his Manchester United team beaten 2-0 by the German club in a pre-season friendly. "Nuremburg are a strong, fast and skilful side and one of the toughest we have faced in Continental football," said the Scot. "Everton will have to work hard, very hard, to get through."

Busby was spot on. There were two goals in the game but it was memorable mainly for the fouls, the retaliation and for reserve keeper Andy Rankin being sent on to treat a player after trainer Tommy Eggleston ran into trouble with the Czech referee. The team was: West, Wright, Wilson, Gabriel, Brown, Harris, Temple, Stevens, Pickering, Harvey, Morrissey.

The game began with a great flurry of football from Everton in which they almost took the lead. Almost straight from the kick-off, they forced a corner. Taken by Johnny Morrissey, the ball fell in the box for Brian Harris whose shot hit the post. There was another chance for the Blues when a bad foul on Fred Pickering led to a free kick which resulted in a chance for Morrissey but he put the ball wide.

Eggleston was to be prominent for Everton, seemingly covering every blade of grass to treat fallen Blues. First there was Pickering then Sandy Brown who took a nasty, bad-tempered kick from Brungs.

The first Blue to retaliate was Jimmy Gabriel who fouled Strehl. The game degenerated into a series of ugly fouls and tit-for-tat retaliation although intermittently Everton produced some fine football. Midway through the first half however the home side took the lead with a diving header from Greif. Brown had slipped as he went to cut out a pass and Alleman had raced down the wing before sending over an excellent cross.

Shortly afterwards Temple was in the wars. He retaliated after being hacked once too often by full back Hilpert. Both were booked but Reisch escaped punishment minutes later when he simply flattened Temple as a throw-in was being made. Temple was able to gain some satisfaction however from his deft part in Everton's equaliser five minutes into the second half. From a corner, he slipped the ball out to Tommy Wright who put over a cross that Harris met superbly to give the keeper no chance. This seemed to rile the Germans further. Brungs was booked for blatantly pushing several Blues players at a corner. Wenauer was the next to have a hack at Temple who must have been viewed as a threat by the Germans.

Then when Greif fouled Wright and the whistle did not blow, the young fullback decided to give him a taste of his own medicine, for which he was booked. On 75 minutes came a madcap moment when Everton had two players laid out on the floor, Harvey in midfield and Morrissey on the edge of the German box. Eggleston ran to Morrissey but just as he got there so too did two German first-aid men and the Nuremburg goalie.

The two stretcher bearers began pulling at Morrissey. Eggleston, fearing that his player may have suffered a broken leg, intervened. The keeper swung a pitch at the Everton trainer who pushed him away. Eggleston said later: "The referee ordered me out of the ground and the goalkeeper picked up my medical bag and hurled it off the pitch." The referee claimed he had not given Eggleston permission to enter the pitch. However the Everton trainer insisted he had waved him on. Eggleston stayed in the stadium following a brief discussion with Nuremburg officials. He re-took his seat on the visitors' bench. But when Wright needed treatment a few minutes later it was Rankin who went on to attend to him.

When the final whistle went it was one goal apiece. But Everton had won on fouls, narrowly, committing 20 to Nuremburg's 16. It was another physically resolute performance by the Blues although it was reported the next day that only three of the team were uninjured. Michael Charters wrote in the Liverpool Echo: "This game became a disgrace to football and made one wonder if European competition is worthwhile ... The Germans started it with late tackles and obstruction and when the Everton players retaliated the result was inevitable - the game became little more than a running battle."

The referee, Dr Gulba, said "The players of both sides were unnecessarily hard and there was too much pushing. In the second half the fouls became too severe altogether." His words beg the question of why he never sent anyone off. Riemke, the technical director of Nuremburg, said both sides were "guilty". He added: "I was surprised at the speed that Everton showed. I did not think they could play like this after watching them against Liverpool last Saturday."

And perhaps there lies a clue to the Everton performance in Germany. The season wasn't going too well, we were mid-table and the previous weekend Everton had been thrashed 5-0 by Liverpool. The Kopites, and those who claimed allegiance to LFC, were beside themselves. With grins on their faces, they would say: "Do you know what the time is? Five past West!" The first time you heard it, you told them to get lost. The second, you admitted, perhaps just to yourself, it was quite funny. But you would hear it another umpteen times; it was painful.

The Everton players would have spent several days at home before flying to Germany, putting up with the jibes from the Reds and moans from the Everton supporters. The players would want to get it out of their system in their next game. So if the German players were a bit physical in Nuremburg, it was perhaps no surprise that the Everton players dished it back.

Before the return, we had two home games in the league. We drew 2-2 with Blackburn with goals from Gabriel and Labone, then beat Tottenham 3-1. Gabriel scored twice and Pickering once. The Germans came to Goodison to defend, hoping to catch Everton on the break. Again they were physical and uncompromising but thankfully lacking the malice displayed in the first leg. Everton worked hard to break down the Nuremburg defence but when they did find a way through, the Blues either wasted their chances or could not beat the keeper Warba who was in brilliant form. Pickering was judged particularly wasteful in front of goal. Gordon West had little to do, but go to hospital. He fell over the Nuremburg striker Bast and fell awkwardly, breaking his collar bone. Rankin was again sent on to the pitch, this time to take over in between the sticks rather than to offer first-aid. West meanwhile was taken to Gateacre Hospital.

The stoppage possibly interrupted Everton's rhythm and their game became a little ragged. Temple and Scott were putting in a stream of crosses but Warba was confident coming out of his goal to meet them and his handling was first class. He also pulled off a great double save from Gabriel and superbly defied Pickering.

Gabriel was also putting himself about, committing several fouls that would have provoked a bust-up in the first leg. But it seemed the Germans were playing to orders as they did not retaliate. Nor did they show much inspiration going forward. The second half was rather similar with Warba keeping Everton at bay, making one astounding save to tip over a Young header. Gabriel headed against the bar and Temple fired over.

The 39,000 crowd was becoming restless but the deadlock was broken midway through the second half. After a cross from Wright, following a short corner by Alex Scott, Harris headed against the bar and Gabriel seized on the rebound to put Everton in front. Everton continued to dominate but they almost paid the price for their failure to beat Warba more than once. With just minutes to go, the Nuremburg wing half Wild, lurking outside the Everton box struck a scorching shot. Rankin had been a virtual spectator but leapt into action, deflecting the flight of the ball so that it skimmed the top of bar. The resulting corner was cleared and Everton held on for a 2-1 aggregate victory. But it had been hard fought. A total of around 40 fouls were awarded by the French referee Marcel Bois who was praised for a no-nonsense approach.

The Everton medical staff were left busy. Not only did they have West's collar bone to contemplate, but the next morning they had to send Labone and Harris for X-rays. The centre half had an injured toe and the half back a problem with his cheekbone. It would have been a disappointing evening for the German players. Cue the Number One single of the time, Tears (For Souvenirs) by Ken Dodd. And after the game they were obliged to attend the formal post-match dinner which was standard practice at the time. Gifts were presented by the home club, with Everton giving Nuremburg a silver cigarette box, presumably for use in the boardroom. Each Nuremburg player was presented with a silver teaspoon. That was stirring it.

Nuremburg went on to win the Bundesliga in 1968, becoming the first club to win the German championship nine times, but then they somehow got themselves relegated the very next season. Nuremburg have never won the title since then. It was as if they failed to get to grips with the re-organisation of the top flight, even though they had previously triumphed in it more than anyone else. It was a huge turning point. As Nuremburg went down in 1969, the Bundesliga was won by Bayern Munich. It was like handing over the crown of Bavaria.

7 UPSY DAISY

Ujpest Dozsa
Inter Cities Fairs Cup
1965-66

It was Everton's first trip behind the Iron Curtain. But what made it a really intriguing prospect was the challenge of playing a Hungarian club. Being drawn in the second round of the Fairs Cup to play Ujpest Dozsa threw up images of the Mighty Magyars, the nickname given to the Hungarian national team that had thrashed England 6-3 in 1953, becoming the first foreign team to beat England at Wembley. A return game had been hastily arranged in Budapest to give England the opportunity to salvage national pride. Hungary won 7-1. The two defeats led to much hand-wringing and soul-searching among the football pundits of the 1950s who endlessly discussed the Hungarians's new tactic of the deep-lying centre-forward, the pioneer being Nandor Hidegkuti, which left the two inside forwards - Kocsis and Puskas - as the main thrust of the attack. It was the beginning of the 4-2-4 and 4-4-2 formations and certainly flummoxed England.

However one major factor overlooked at the time was that in both games there was not one Everton player in the England team. A rule of thumb, which became more apparent in 1966, 1970 and 1986, is that England only ever have a prayer when Everton are doing well. But Hungary were blessed with a generation of superbly skilful footballers and the political system at the time was conducive to maximising those talents.

Following the end of the Second World War, many countries in Eastern Europe came under the control of the Union of Soviet Socialist Republics (USSR), run from the Kremlin in the Russian capital Moscow. In keeping with the logic of soviets - workers' councils - the authorities encouraged team identities to be based less on localities and more on aspects of the workers' state. Teams named Torpedo were of the car-building and truck industry; Red Star denoted sports clubs of the national army; Lokomotiv were teams of the railway sector. Dynamo was a name usually given to teams of the Interior Ministry or secret police. One can only imagine what names would have applied to English clubs if the Russians had ever taken over here. Given our post-war dip in fortunes, we may have become Torpedoed Everton. In actual fact, one British club did adopt a Soviet-style prefix although it wasn't until the tailend of the Cold War that a North Wales slatetown club with a sense of humour renamed itself Locomotive Llanberis.

But in the Eastern Bloc this politicisation of football clubs was further corrupted by the tendency of the most powerful, notably the army, to poach the best players. The Hungarian army took over the Kispest club - fortuitously inheriting Puskas - and in 1948 renamed the club Honved. Under the guise of National Service call-ups, they poached the country's best players.

Our opponents had started in 1885 as Ujpest Torna Egylet, the gymnastics club of Ujpest, which is a district of Budapest, but the football section did not kick off until 1900. They eventually became the dominant force in Hungarian football, winning the championship five times in the 1930s and three times straight after the war, 1945-47, but then came Honved who became the dominant force.

Ujpest became the team of the Interior Ministry who in 1949, not content with the name of a suburb, gave the club the grander sounding and politically correct name of Budapesti Dozsa, after the capital city and Gyorgy Dozsa, who had led a peasant revolt more than 400 years earlier. Dozsa had been captured and grilled alive; doubtless, while rotating on the spit it would have been some consolation to him that a footy team would be named after him.

Dozsa remained a formidable footballing force in the 1950s but Honved conscripted the best players into its football training camps and became the most highly rated club side in Europe until 1956 when there was a rebellion on the streets of Hungary which was crushed by Russian tanks. Honved were on tour and some of their players, such as Puskas, decided not to return home.

It was also in 1956 that Budapesti Dozsa was re-renamed Ujpest Dozsa. With Honved no longer invincible, Ujpest won the championship in 1960 for the first time in 13 years. Throughout the Sixties, the Hungarians continued to place great emphasis on technical skill. Spectators at the 1966 World Cup games at Goodison Park were to be enthralled by the play of the Hungarian team, notably Florian Albert of Ferencvaros and Ferenc Bene of Ujpest, who had been leading goalscorer in the 1964 Olympics in which Hungary won the gold medal in football. No, Everton were not involved in the build-up.

It was clear that Everton would need to be at their best in Budapest. So there was some concern when it emerged that Harry Catterick would have to miss the trip due to illness. Left in charge of the team was the trainer Tommy Eggleston. Of course, today he would have been described as the assistant coach. He took a 15-man squad that comprised the team that started against Blackburn the previous Saturday - with the exception of Jimmy Gabriel who had picked up an injury - plus Sandy Brown, Dennis Stevens, reserve keeper Geoff Barnett, 19-year-old Gerry Glover and 18-year-old Jimmy Husband.

The Everton party had a tortuous journey, staying in a Manchester hotel on Sunday night then flying early the next morning to Brussels then to Cologne and on to Budapest where they were driven to their hotel.

"I remember being in that hotel in Budapest because there was an interpreter who was trying to tell us that we had to go and meet someone," said Brian Labone. "He told us to look for a fella who was 5ft tall, fat and had a limp with a moustache. It might not sound funny now but Ray Wilson and I were in stitches and still laugh about it now."

It was to have been an afternoon kick-off because Ujpest's stadium had no floodlights. But the game was switched to the national stadium with a 5.30pm kick-off. It was reported that this was due to the Hungarian FA wanting the game to be televised live. If so, it was possibly the first time Everton had a kick-off time changed due to the demands of television. The team was: Rankin, Wright, Wilson, Stevens, Labone, Harris, Scott, Harvey, Pickering, Temple, Morrissey.

Ten days earlier Everton coach Ron Lewin had travelled to Hungary to watch Ujpest so the Blues had a good idea of what to expect. The Blues began by getting men behind the ball but the Hungarian trickery, both on and off the ball, was to be too much. Johnny Morrissey did have a chance in the opening minutes after breaking free but his shot went over the bar. Ujpest had their first clear chance on goal after nine minutes and it fell to Egor Solymosi, a big, strapping wing half with a deft touch and a powerful shot to which he could add a vicious swerve. His shot from outside the box was said to have hit the net while Andy Rankin was still airborne.

The ball control and passing of Ujpest was clearly from the mould of the Magyars. Midway through the first half, Solymosi undid Everton again. He took a free kick from outside the box and hit it low and hard. It beat Rankin but Tommy Wright was on the line and blocked the shot. However the ball fell to 20-year-old Bene who slotted it home from close range.

It was 2-0 at half-time and the Blues were facing their first heavy defeat in Europe. The Hungarians' control and passing was a joy to watch but sadly there was only around 5,000 spectators in the ground. From a typical piece of interplay between Bene and Gorocs, Zambo was given the space to put over a cross which struck a blue shirt. The ball fell to the impressive Kuharsky who shot into the roof of the net to make it 3-0. The Hungarians seemed to take their foot off the pedal after that. But still they had two good opportunities to score, both falling to Bene. After an Everton attack broke down, Ujpest broke away and Bene was put clear but as Rankin came out of his goal, the young Hungarian shot wide. With a few minutes to go, Bene was one on one with Rankin again, but this time the keeper pulled off a fine save to stop a strong goalbound shot.

Fred Pickering had scored against all of the three teams Everton had played in Europe last season, but had not found the Nuremburg net and he was given little leeway in Hungary, although he did win the ball in the air to create chances for Brian Harris and Derek Temple but their efforts were to no avail.

Labone was impressed by the Hungarians. He recalled: "Bene gave me a hard time although I did not have a particularly bad game. But he was very mobile and so skilful. The other thing was their players interchanged a lot so that you never knew who you were supposed to be marking. Also it was one of these teams that seemed to contain half the national side; that was their strength, they were always so used to playing as a team."

The arduous travelling may have taken its toll on the players as the following Saturday Everton lost 2-1 at home to Leicester in front of a crowd of 30,000. The next Saturday they travelled to Sheffield United and lost 2-0, leaving the Blues in 13th position in the table.

On a very cold November night, around 24,000 Evertonians witnessed what was very much a footballing masterclass by the Hungarians. Pronouncing the name Ujpest Dozsa was a problem for many Evertonians who instead referred to them as "Upsy Daisy", but that did not stop them appreciating the fine football played that evening. The Everton team was: Rankin, Wright, Wilson, Harvey, Labone, Harris, Temple, Gabriel, Young, Husband, Morrissey.

The Blues made a great start, scoring in just four minutes with a header by Harris, raising hopes of a sensational comeback. Alex Young and Morrissey were rising to the occasion and showing the Hungarians that they could play a bit too. Harris and Colin Harvey were industrious. But there was more guile from the Hungarians who played with elegance and an air of assurance. And on the half-hour an equaliser came from the winger Lenkei. At half-time it was 1-1 on the night and 4-1 on aggregate to "Upsy Daisy".

Everton pressed hard in the second half and enjoyed a great deal of possession, with Morrissey, Temple and Husband all working hard to find a way through. But the Hungarians repelled with steely grace. They were dangerous on the counter-attack. But the only goal in the second half was an own goal which came in the closing stages when the defender Nosko turned a cross from Temple into his own net. It gave Everton a 2-1 aggregate on the night but it was 4-2 to "Upsy Daisy" on aggregate.

A few years later Ujpest were to take a special place in the hearts of Geordies. The Hungarian club reached the Fairs Cup final but lost over two legs to Newcastle. It was the last trophy Newcastle won in the 20th century. Ujpest consoled themselves with the Hungarian double in 1969 and won the title eight times in the 1970s. In 1991, following the fall of state communism, Újpest dropped the word Dozsa from their name. Today they still play in the top flight of Hungarian football.

8. THE BOYS OF '66

Aalborg
European Cup Winners Cup
1966-67

Mike Trebilcock only played 15 games for Everton and scored just five goals, but they included two goals in one of the most famous matches in the club's history, the 1966 FA Cup final. It was one of the most dramatic finals seen at Wembley, with Everton coming from 2-0 down to beat Sheffield Wednesday, but was quickly overshadowed by another game played at Wembley a few weeks later - the World Cup final in which England defeated West Germany 4-2. Understandably "The Boys of 66" have gone down in history: West, Wright, Wilson, Gabriel, Labone, Harris, Scott, Young, Trebilcock, Harvey, Temple.

Nor should we forget Fred Pickering who had been troubled with a knee complaint and desperately wanted to play but Harry Catterick, concerned about his sharpness, left him out of the team, selecting instead Trebilcock who scored twice. Big Fred was also unlucky not to be in the World Cup squad. When Everton travelled to Denmark for their first ever game in the European Cup Winners Cup, Pickering was still sidelined, with Trebilcock taking his place.

Their opponents were Aalborg who remain today a club which sporadically challenges the supremacy in Denmark of the Copenhagen teams. Accordingly, Aalborg supporters proclaim their team as the Pride of Northern Jutland, a description possibly fuelled by the town's production of Schnapps. This would have been flowing in '66 when Aalborg won the Danish Cup for the first time in their history which began in 1885 when English railway workers in Denmark formed a cricket club. For something to do in the winter they formed a football team. The cricket club was still going strong in the 1960s, so much so that in 1966 it won the Danish cricket championship for the sixth successive year. Aalborg football team however were not to win the Danish football championshp until 1995 when they became the first club from Denmark to compete in the European Champions League. But back in 1966 the Danish footballing authorities were clinging tenaciously to the amateur ethos. Consequently, Denmark's best players had to move to foreign clubs if they wanted to earn a living from the game. And they did produce some good players, as indicated by the 1960 Olympics in which Denmark won the silver medal in football.

Accordingly in September 1966, Evertonians were expecting their Danish opponents, many of whom held down full-time jobs, to be rather similar to the Norwegian team they had faced in Oslo two years earlier. In fact, the Danes were to give the Blues a tougher time. Everton's form was cavalier. Their last game at Goodison before flying to Denmark had been a glorious goal-feast in which the Blues beat West Brom 5-4, with two goals from a new idol, Alan Ball. Catterick had paid Blackpool a record £110,000 for the 21-year-old who had been a star of England's World Cup triumph.

This led again to Everton being described as the Mersey Millionaires and a growing belief that John Moores was delving into his personal fortune to buy players for Everton. Moores helped the club immensely but, as we have seen, he was making the club interest-free loans. Perhaps one should not rule out the possibility that he may have occasionally donated money to the club, or even that he told the club not to bother repaying a loan. But I doubt it. He was said to be a very thrifty, parsimonius man, reportedly even buying shoes from catalogues, so throwing money at a football club would have been out of character.

Only a detailed examination of the club's accounts might provide an undisputed answer. But consider this crude analysis of the transfer fees throughout the Sixties. Based on these figures, the club paid out a total of £892,500 and recouped £474,500 in sales.

IN: 1960 - Vernon, £27,000; Lill, £25,000; Gabriel, £30,000; Bingham, £15,000; Young, £45,000; Thomson, £15,000. 1961 - Veall, £7,500; Heslop, unable to establish. 1962 - West, £28,000; Stevens, £32,000; Kay, £55,000; Morrissey, £10,000. 1963 - Scott, £40,000; Hill, £25,000; Brown, £38,000. 1964 - Pickering, £85,000; Wilson, £35,000. 1965 - Trebilcock, £20,000. 1966 - Ball, £110,000. 1967 - Hunt, £80,000; Kendall, £80,000. 1969 - K.Newton, £90,000. TOTAL - £892,500

OUT: 1960 - J.Harris, £20,000. 1961 - Collins, £30,000. 1962 - Lill, £12,5000; Wignall, £20,000; Green, £12,000. 1963 - Bingham, unable to establish; Thomson, unable to establish. 1964 - Hill, unable to establish. 1965: Heslop, £20,000; Stevens, £20,000; Vernon, £40,000; Veall, unable to establish. 1966: B.Harris, £15,000. 1967 - Gabriel, £45,000; Pickering, £50,000; Trebilcock, £35,000; Scott, £15,000; Temple, £35,000; 1968: Hunt, £70,000; 1969 - Barnett, £35,000. TOTAL - £474,500.

The figures are from published sources which sometimes vary a little. Excluded are players who figure as the makeweight in a part-exchange, for instance, when Ray Wilson was signed, Everton paid

£35,000 to Huddersfield who also received Mick Meagan. The list is not exhaustive. It does not include players who had come through the youth ranks, made a few appearances, then moved on to other clubs, possibly for a small fee. Such players include Bobby Laverick, Brian Godfrey, Barrie Rees, Roy Parnell, George Sharples, Derek Smith, Stuart Shaw, Gerry Glover and Aidan Maher. So the total figures of around £892,000 and £474,000 should be seen only as an approximate, but still useful as a basis for discussion.

The difference between transfer fees paid out and received is £418,000, approximately, an average annual outlay of £42,000 a year. Where did we get the money to cover that yearly deficit? As early as 1962-63, gate receipts were as high as £190,000. The average attendance that season was 51,000, but admission prices would go up as the Sixties progressed and the average attendance over the decade was 45,000. Also take into account the additional revenue from two FA Cup runs to Wembley and the share of the receipts that one might reasonably assume we got from being the second most used venue in the 1966 World Cup finals.

And bear in mind that for most of the 1960s, if not all, most players' wages were not that much greater than those paid to the man in the street. Sandy Brown has said that when he joined Everton in 1963 he was delighted with the wages, £25 per week, although he may have been excluding bonuses. In 1962-63, the club paid £67,000 in wages. If that was divided between a first-team squad of 17, it would work out at an average of £4,000 a year, or £80 a week. But of course there were a lot more than 17 players on the books.

So, taking the 1962-63 figures, subtract £67,000 for wages from the gate receipts of £190,000 and there is £123,000 left. Deduct the average transfer outlay of £42,000 and that still leaves £81,000. Of course, there were team travelling expenses, stadium maintenance amd miscellaneous costs, but Everton Football Club looked to be self-sufficient.

This perhaps raises the question of why Moores did not correct the journalists who kept on portraying him as the club's sugar daddy? It has to be borne in mind that Moores was a private man who only spoke to the press when he felt it was necessary. It had been made clear at AGMs that he was loaning the club money, not donating. If some reporters got this wrong, why should he worry about it? The misconception reflected well on him and took pressure off him. If Evertonians thought he was not actually writing out cheques from his own bank account, then they might demand that he did.

Finally, see what Jim Greenwood had to say before retiring as club secretary. In a revealing series of interviews with Ken Rogers of the Liverpool Echo in 1993, Greenwood praised Moores highly but said: "He never put millions into the club as is widely assumed by many supporters. Indeed, the most he ever loaned was the cash to finance the new floodlights - and even that was a very controlled business arrangement."

This point about Moores is raised not to denigrate the man in any way. But his contribution should be seen in the right context, for it serves no useful purpose for Evertonians to labour under misconceptions about finance, thinking that we once had a blue Santa Claus and that another might one day be found to solve the club's financial woes.

The loans would have been a big help to the club, giving the Blues an edge in the transfer market, especially in the early 60s, ultimately leading to the championship success of 1963. But there was something else that Moores loaned to Everton - his business skills. He was a man with vision and he could see a better way for the club to obtain quality players, a better value way: a renewed emphasis on youth development. And so the club spent £25,000 on the Bellefield training ground. Once the facilities were in place, it was considered by many to be the best in the land.

He also used his business skills to help Everton in negotiations and in strategic approaches to the challenges ahead. And it might not be unreasonable to assume that Moores sometimes deployed Littlewoods resources, such as the expertise of a lawyer, to help the club solve problems that cropped up, thus saving Everton money.

This was done out of altruism, wanting to help. He never wanted to make money out of Everton. So what was in it for him? A sense of satisfaction at seeing the club maximise its commercial potential, and delight when the team did well, I would suggest.

Greenwood told Rogers in that 1993 interview: "What he (Moores) did give us was his name and the power that goes with running a very successful business. It opened doors at the bank whenever we wanted to finance a big deal."

When the 1966-67 season kicked off, Goodison Park was the centre of attention as it was the venue for the curtain-raising Charity Shield match. Before the game, Wilson, widely considered at the time to be the world's best left-back, and Liverpool's Roger Hunt, who had both played for England in the World Cup final, did a lap of honour with the Jules Rimet trophy, the FA Cup and the League Championship which Liverpool had won. Unfortunately the Reds went home with the Charity Shield after a 1-0 win, but in the third league game of the season we beat them 3-1 with two goals from Ball and one from Brown in front of another capacity crowd of 64,000.

Our trip to Denmark made us the second English team - Manchester United were the first - to compete in all three European competitions. As soon as the team arrived in Aalborg on the day before the game, Catterick had the players out for a training session at their modern stadium.

There had been a change in the rules which allowed goalkeepers to be substituted and so Andy Rankin had travelled with the team, along with two other reserves, Brown and Alex Scott. But the convivial surroundings were to be the setting for a dour game as the Danes decided to give their 15,000 supporters an exhibition of all-out defence. The Everton strike force of Alex Young and Trebilcock, both only 5ft 8ins and of slender frame, found themselves running into defenders much taller and stronger. The power of Pickering was sorely missed. The Everton team was: West, Wright, Wilson, Gabriel, Labone, Harvey, Temple, Ball, Young, Trebilcock, Morrissey.

It proved an inauspicious start to European club competition for Ball, who worked hard in midfield. He also popped up in the penalty box to direct a goalbound header that forced a good save from the home keeper Sorenson. Trebilcock had chances to be a cup hero again but put a header over the bar and shot wide when the best chance of the game fell to him. It was his one and only game in European competition for the Blues. The game finished goalless and it meant the Danes still had a chance of sneaking past their famous opponents into the next round, particularly if they could score an away goal at Goodison.

The Cup Winners Cup at this time carried more prestige than the Fairs Cup in many people's eyes. This was partly due to the peculiar history of the Fairs Cup and its idiosyncracies such as the one-city rule which was soon to bedevil the Blues. The Cup Winners Cup was for teams who had won a trophy, although beaten finalists would be entered when a team had done the double and opted instead for the more prestigious European Cup. For instance, Leicester City entered the 1961-62 tournament after losing the FA Cup final to the 1961 double-winning Spurs side.

Before joining Everton, Scott had scored in the first Cup Winners Cup final when Rangers lost a two-legged affair 4-1 on aggregate to Fiorentina in 1961. Only 10 clubs had entered that inaugural competition, including Wolves who beat FK Austria and were straight into the semi-finals, losing to Rangers. The number of entrants the following season was 23, with nine clubs receiving byes into the second round. Leicester overcame Glenavon but went out to Atletico Madrid.

The 1962 final, in which Atletico beat Fiorentina, saw the start of the Cup Winners Cup jinx. No club ever won the trophy in two successive seasons, even though eight holders of the trophy got to the final the following year. Atletico lost in the 1963 final to Spurs. The other six holders to lose the following season's final were AC Milan, Anderlecht, Ajax, Parma, Arsenal and Paris St Germain. When the Cup Winners Cup was played for the last time in 1999, it had been going for 39 seasons yet not one club had managed to retain it.

Everton were under a little extra pressure in the tournament in 1966 because in three of the previous four seasons English clubs had reached the Cup Winners Cup final. After Tottenham's triumph, Bobby Moore's West Ham had won the 1965 tournament and Liverpool had reached the final in 1966 but lost in extra-time at Hampden Park to Borussia Dortmund.

After Liverpool's promotion to the First Division in 1962, they had quickly established themselves as a formidable force. They were so good they were nearly as good as us. But what was truly remarkable was how quickly they became fashionable. It was "cool" to support Liverpool. Why should this have been so? Between 1963 and 1966, Everton had won two trophies to Liverpool's three, but this slight edge in silverware was not the explanation. There were two factors: Bill Shankly and media glorification of the Kop.

Shankly was the first person I ever disliked intensely. I was only a child but he kept on upsetting me. It was the comments he made - "If Everton were playing at the bottom of the garden, I'd draw the curtains," and "There's only two teams in Liverpool; Liverpool and Liverpool Reserves".

In defence of Shankly, Peter Barnes - then a teenage Kopite but someone who in middle-age had a picture of Shankly on his office wall - said: "Those things were said tongue-in-cheek, with humour, and partly to motivate his own team."

That may be true, but those remarks were to be repeated time and time again, tediously, by the growing band of Reds. My dislike was to dissipate over the years. I realised that when the Liverpool board appointed Shankly as manager, they could not have realised they were also getting a public relations genius. With his one-liners, infectious enthusiasm and apparent willingness to talk all day, he was a godsend to journalists always looking for a fresh line. Our Harry, on the other hand, tended to keep his thoughts to himself. Just like Moores, the man who had appointed him, Catterick was a naturally quiet man who enjoyed privacy. Talking to journalists was a chore for Catterick, something he would do if he must, but he would rather let his team do his talking for him on the pitch, which they usually did very well. But away from match days, journalists generally found it easier to get a story relating to Liverpool. The column inches stacked up.

And then there was the Kop. It was in something like 1964 that a BBC man returned to London with footage, still shown every now and again, of the Kop swaying, surging, singing a Beatles song - She Loves You, I think. In this footage the Beeb man speaks excitedly in his Home Counties accent of his discovery, as if he were an anthropologist who has just discovered a tribe of nine-throated humans. This kickstarted a media fascination with the Kop which would become famous the world over.

Initially the Kop was a natural phenomenon, a product of Merseyside boisterousness and wit. Those who stood on this huge slab of terracing came from exactly the same background as those who watched their football at Goodison Park. So why did we not have something of similar allure?

The explanation lies in design. The most important factor was that the Kop had a roof that covered all the spectators. When they sang, it echoed. At Goodison, the chants of many Blues standing behind the goals disappeared into thin air because there was no roof above them. There were supporters behind the goals who were under cover - the cover provided by the seating areas above them. But look at the Gwladys Street end today. The upper stand is some considerable distance from the goal - around 25 yards. In the 1960s the only cover for standing spectators at this end was underneath what is now known as the Upper Gwladys Street stand. It was to be another 20 years or so before the roof was extended to cover all spectators. The situation was similar at the smaller Park End, although there the old stand was closer to the pitch. Of course, Evertonians made a huge din at times but, due to the laws of physics, a lot of it was dissipated.

Nor was the crowd at Goodison breathing down the backs of the goalnets, as they did at the Kop. In the early Sixties, after a dart was thrown at the Tottenham keeper Bill Brown, Everton were ordered to alter the terracing so that supporters were a minimum distance away from the goals. Hence Goodison ended up with a curved wall behind the goals. These arcs looked stylish, even avant-garde, almost as if they were from a John Moores art exhibition, and many visitors found them aesthetically appealing. But in keeping spectators away from the goals, they detracted from the intensity of the atmosphere.

Nor could the eye-catching surges of Kopites be replicated behind the goals at Goodison. The Park End was not that big while the larger Gwladys Street terracing was two-tier in that there was a lower standing area and a higher standing area which was on a ledge. There were surges but they could only go so far.

Also, the basic nature of Anfield lent itself to a greater sense of community. My dad took me to one game at Anfield, in the mid-Sixties, against Leicester who won 1-0, if that is not wishful thinking. Sitting in one of the two stands, it seemed rather grey to me, although it was probably a damp, dreary day. I don't see how anybody could have got above their station in life in that place, even if they were sitting in the seats. Goodison on the other hand was rather grand in the 1960s, with the blue criss-cross panelling on the stands giving the place an almost aristocratic air. There were four stands looking down on four terraces. The criss-cross panelling remains on two sides of the ground today but sadly is hidden behind advertising boards.

The aesthetics of Goodison Park won it many admirers, especially with the four sides being similar in style. Remember that it was the most used club ground in the 1966 World Cup finals, hosting the semi-final between West Germany and Russia. But the bog standard nature of Anfield was more conducive to noise and wave-like crowd movements. Then of course the word "Kop", only three letters, lent itself to newspaper headlines, unlike "Gwladys Street", never a snappy, sexy name. Increasingly, there was a trendiness about being a "Kopite". I was frequently baffled how the Kop fitted on all the people who claimed they had stood there the previous Saturday.

A classic example of the lure of the Kop is Tony O'Neill, one of five brothers from Bootle. Aged 10 at the time of the Aalborg game, he said: "My dad was an Evertonian, my two oldest brothers were Blues, the next two were Liverpool supporters and then there was me. My dad took me to Goodison and I thought this is great. I always remember my first game was the one against Leeds where the referee took the players off the pitch for 10 minutes because of all the fouling.

"Then one of my Red brothers took me to watch Liverpool and I thought this is even better. It seemed more colourful and a better atmosphere. I suppose the thing was we stood in the Anfield Road and looked over at the Kop and all the scarves being raised in the air. That was 1969," added O'Neill, who today is an Anfield season ticket holder.

Barnes said: "Liverpool were the ascendant team. After promotion in 1962, there was the league championship in 1964 and the FA Cup in 1965, which I attended, and then it went on from there. In my teenage years, I was very much taken with it all. It was something to be proud of; just to say you were a Liverpool supporter was like a badge of honour. And of course there was the whole Beatles thing. I was 18 in 1965 and Liverpool was the pop cultural capital of the world. I would go away with the lads, some of whom were Evertonians of course, camping, whatever, and we would be the centre of attraction with the girls and the other groups of people. We came from Liverpool, this special place, home of great football and the Beatles - and we milked it for all it was worth."

When Everton ran out for the second leg at Goodison there was an air of expectancy, but what was not expected was that Aalborg would employ exactly the same tactics as they did in the first leg: all-out defence. And again Everton had nobody up front with a physical presence to worry the powerful Danish defenders. Jimmy Husband, a few days away from his 19th birthday, was making his first appearance of the season and doing his best to link up with Young. Johnny Morrissey on the wing had aggression in abundance but was unlikely to outjump the tall Danes when he got into the box. When crosses were floated into the box, the Danes easily took care of them. As the teams trooped in at half-time there was an element of head-scratching about how the Blues were going to prise open the visitors' defence. Two and a quarter hours of football had passed and we still had not scored against the amateurs.

The second leg was approaching its 60-minute mark when the Blues finally scored. Ball swung over a corner, Jimmy Gabriel headed it down and the ball fell to Morrissey who poked it home. Aalborg made few attacks of note in the whole game but stunned the crowd by equalising. After a long-range shot by Neilsen was saved by Gordon West, the Danes had a rare corner and the ball found its way to Lildballe who, standing just a few yards out, gleefully netted. The scoreline meant that Everton were going out of the competition on the away goals rule. This would be a major shock in the next day's newspapers and a massive embarrassment for Everton.

A few minutes later however Young played a delightful ball for Morrissey who took the ball to almost the goalline and squared it for Ball to knock home from close range. The Danes were not happy, particularly Larsen who was booked for a foul on Harvey then put in a bad challenge on Ball that prompted the referee to send him off. Despite playing against 10 men, we held on for the 2-1 win.

9. LOS MAGNIFICOS

Real Zaragoza
European Cup Winners Cup
1966-67

The draw for the second round gave Everton their first tie against a club that had won a European trophy. Real Zaragoza remain to this day an enigma of Spanish football. Located midway between Madrid and Barcelona, they have often proved their mettle by beating the grand teams of those two famous cities. But somehow, even to this day, they have never managed to win the Spanish championship despite assembling some great sides. One of these was the team of the mid-60s, fondly recalled by their supporters who still enthuse about Los Magníficos, which refers to the forward line of of Canario, Santos, Marcelino, Villa and Lapetra.

This team had made their mark in Europe, winning the Fairs Cup in 1964 and reaching the final of the tournament again in 1966, only to lose to Barcelona. But Zaragoza had beaten Athletic Bilbao 2-0 in the 1966 Spanish Cup final. It was the fourth successive season they had reached the final. The previous year Atletico Madrid had gained revenge for Zaragoza's triumph over them in the 1964 final. Zaragoza had lost the 1963 final to Barcelona.

Everton travelled to Spain for the first leg in great spirits, unbeaten in 12 games with wins from their last five matches which had put them third in the league behind Chelsea and Stoke. Catterick warned his players however to expect a difficult game. "Zaragoza have a tough tackling defence and a brilliant attack, as good as any in Europe when they are on form," he said.

On the day before the game, the Everton players trained at Bellefield then boarded a coach that took them to Liverpool Airport for a chartered flight that, after stopping at Bordeaux, landed in heavy rain at a NATO airfield near Zaragoza. Waiting there was local football journalist Ricardo Gil of the Hearaldo de Aragon. He told his readers: "At the airport we spoke to Harry Catterick, manager of the club. Not a great deal though since he was not in a talkative mood."

Gil then recounted their conversation in which Catterick was actually quite sociable, I thought, for someone who had just got off a plane and wanted to get to his hotel. He showed some humour too. Asked, among other things, if he had decided on his line-up yet, Catterick replied: "No, sir. I've brought 14 players but I'll only be picking 11. Don't worry!"

Nor did the sartorial style of our players meet with Gil's approval. "Despite being genuine compatriots of The Beatles, they were all wearing the frighteningly classical grey," he told his readers.

Our Fab Fourteen were then driven to the hotel where the Spanish club held a reception and banquet. On the morning of the game the squad visited the 35,000 capacity La Romareda stadium, which had only opened in 1957, before returning to their hotel to prepare themselves for the test ahead. Zaragoza were lying fourth in the Spanish league, having lost at home a few days earlier to Barcelona. Watching that game were Everton scouts Harry Cooke and Arthur Proudler. In addition, Catterick had spoken to Leeds manager Don Revie about the Spanish team because just six months earlier the

Yorkshire club had lost a three-legged Fairs Cup semi-final to the Spaniards. In a televised play-off, English football fans had seen a dazzling display of attacking football from Zaragoza.

Officially Real Zaragoza had been founded in 1932, when the local teams Iberia S.C. and Real Zaragoza C.D., said to be exhausted by years of fierce rivalry, decided to merge in an attempt to give the city of Zaragoza one major club. This may have been prompted by the formation a few years earlier, in 1928, of the Spanish League. A few years earlier, in 1924, Everton had been paid £1,000 by Barcelona to travel there and play two games against them. We won one game 2-1 and lost the other by the same score. Newcastle were also invited and we beat them in Barcelona 3-2. In one of the lounges at Goodison is a trophy which was presented to the team.

Zaragoza started well in the Spanish League with a very talented team known as Los Alifantes, but the outbreak of the Civil War in 1936 led to the suspension of the Spanish League for three years, wreaking havoc with their careers.

In the first 70 seasons of the Spanish championship, only nine clubs had won the title. All but ten of the titles had been won by four clubs: Real Madrid, 28 times; Barcelona, 15; Atlético Madrid, 9, and Athletic Bilbao, 8. The best position that Zaragoza managed was 2nd in 1975 when they finished 12 points behind Real Madrid. But the closest they came to winning the title was in 1965 - a year before our game - when they finished seven points behind the champions, in third place. The Spanish Cup competition had started in 1902 and the same four clubs had enjoyed the lion's share of glory. Zaragoza's cup triumph in 1964 was their first.

The "Magnificos" team was arguably the best Zaragoza ever had. In the eight seasons from 1960 to 1968 they finished in the top five every season, a feat the club has never repeated. While Marcelino and Laperta from the strikeforce had played for Spain in the 1966 World Cup finals in England, the defence had three Spanish internationals in Severino Reija, Violeta and Santamaria.

With Everton and Zaragoza boasting some wonderfully talented players, one might have expected a footballing feast. While there were some great flashes of football there was an ugly side to the game which exploded in a three-minute spell shortly before half-time when the ball was not kicked, but Alex Scott was booked, Gordon West was chased by three Zaragoza players and Johnny Morrissey sent off. The Everton team was: West, Wright, Wilson, Gabriel, Labone, Harvey, Scott, Ball, Young, Temple, Morrissey.

The game began with the Magnificent Five showing their class with some great passing. But their teammates seemed to have targeted Scott and Alan Ball for some fierce tackling. The Zaragoza pressure paid off when Santos headed them into the lead. But then Scott was brought down for the fourth time in 20 minutes, he picked up the ball and threw it at the offender, Lapetra. On the other side of the pitch, the Zaragoza right-half was rolling on the floor. Nearby was Morrissey who looked up to see several Spanish players running over to him. West raced out to intervene and was punched by a Real player. "The game threatened to develop into one of the greatest punch-ups ever seen on a football field," wrote Michael Charters in the Liverpool Echo. Whether it was due to the dismissal of Morrissey, the referee somehow regained a semblance of control.

Enjoy the excerpts from the Heraldo report: "Zaragoza last night were quite different from the team that played last Sunday ... Barcelona's tough defence was a bed of roses compared to Everton's ... Zaragoza started off attacking and weaving patterns against an Everton defence who played a cautious game closing ranks whilst demonstrating great technical ability on the ball.

It was a fine contest that had the crowd on its feet, usually with Zaragoza's movement, but occasionally with the English counter-attacks which threatened danger .... The match had everything - even hitting and punches thrown. The first blows were discreetly done but it culminated in an unseemly free-for-all just before half-time with the English left-winger Morrissey, the instigator and protagonist of the scuffle, heading for the dressing room ... The second half was a transformation. Everton, with a man fewer, resolutely, almost mechanically, decided to shut up shop and defend their goal."

The Spaniards were going for the second goal necessary for a reasonably comfortable cushion in the second leg. However Derek Temple twice broke away on enterprising runs. The first ended with strong penalty appeals when he was brought down by Santamaria but the Swiss referee Hober, said to be 40 yards away, waved play on. Temple's second solo raid on the Zaragoza defence was ended by a fine tackle by Violeta.

The Blues defended superbly, conceding only one goal in the second half when Marcelino headed home midway through the second half. The game finished 2-0. Brian Labone recalled: "They were a very good team but they really kicked us about. They had a centre half called Santamaria - it wasn't the one that played for Real Madrid - who was about 6ft 10ins and he was a right dirty so-and-so."

On the dismissal of Morrissey, which Labone could only vaguely recall, the centre-half said: "John was no ballerina. If he got kicked, he gave a bit back."

The Heraldo told of how the Spanish press tried to get some reaction from the Everton party who apparently spent more than 45 minutes locked in the dressing room after the game. "We called to them several times, we asked for their comments but without success. They came out in single file with deadpan expressions and their heads lowered. I called out to Catterick and tried to speak to him. He did not even look at me; he just ignored me and walked towards the bus, absorbed in self-thought and carried on, as the players had before him, with a blank look on his face staring at no particular object. They were not fond of losing."

The Heraldo added: "We will see if the Everton attack is as dangerous at home as the glimpses we saw of them here in their counter-attacks. We must suppose that they'll be awesome at home ... Zaragoza will have a struggle on their hands."

The game had been watched by the manager of the national Spain team, Domingo Balmanya, who said: "Zaragoza will have to fight hard in Liverpool to hold onto this lead. I think Everton are a better side than suggested by their performance tonight."

Also in the crowd was Edmundo Suárez, coach of Valencia, who said: "Zaragoza deserved more goals because they went out to score three or four, but it's easier said than done to dish out a hiding to a team of Everton's class."

Everton flew back to Liverpool the next day to prepare for a home match against Arsenal 48 hours later on the Saturday. There were many cuts and bruises among the players, but all were fit to play the Gunners. It was to be another tough game as Arsenal decided to come for a point. Their rugged team, featuring strong defensive players such as Frank McLintock, Peter Storey, Ian Ure and Terry Neill, kept the Blues at bay and rarely threatened West at the other end. It was sorely clear that the Blues were missing the physical strength of Pickering who was making slow progress from his cartilage operation. Morrissey limped off on the half-hour after pulling a hamstring. Derek Smith, a strongly built local lad, went on as a substitute and put in several shots and headers but was unable to beat Jim Furnell in goal. Dropping a point, Everton slipped to fourth, while Liverpool went second.

After the Arsenal game, Ray Wilson, Ball and Labone joined the England squad for a midweek international against Wales. Fred Pickering's injury was causing concern. Catterick said: "Fred's progress is rather slow because it must be remembered that his suspect knee broke down twice before it was decided a cartilage operation was necessary. This meant that the knee was exceptionally sore when the operation was decided on."

Travelling to Britain for a game held no fears for Real Zaragoza. They had played 16 ties in European competition and almost half had been against clubs from Britain and Ireland. They had overcome not only Leeds, but also Dundee, Hearts, Dunfermline, Cardiff and Shamrock Rovers. It might explain to some extent why they got "stuck in" so much against Everton. The only team from the British Isles to have knocked out Zaragoza was Bobby Moore's West Ham. That had been two seasons earlier when the Hammers had edged past Zaragoza in the semi-final of the 1964-65 Cup Winners Cup before going on to beat TSV Munich 1860 in the final.

The Spaniards flew into Liverpool on the Monday night, 48 hours before the game. Reporting from Liverpool for the Heraldo was special correspondent Jose Maria Donate who phoned over an article, setting the scene for newspaper readers in Zaragoza. "The hotel window from where I am writing this report is on the fourth floor which is quite high up in this typically English city where most of the houses are built in the Italian Renaissance style of three-storey buildings with shiny slate rooves almost permanently damp ... It is four o'clock and getting dark. Right under my window is a huge bus depot which is, of course, quite full. From here I have a great view of both cathedrals, each one fabulous in its different ways."

I would guess he was in the Adelphi Hotel, overlooking the former Skelhorne Street bus depot, but I am not sure that from his window he could also see the cathedrals. As for the stylish houses, he may have been referring to Seymour Street, Rodney Street and Hope Street areas.

Donate claimed the Spanish party had received a cold welcome: "No Everton official has yet appeared at the hotel ... Only the club secretary was at the airport to greet us. As if the lack of attention was not enough, the Zaragoza players went to Goodison Park to train this morning and they were not allowed in. They were taken instead to one of the many public parks with shabby changing rooms and rudimentary facilities. And it is so cold - today it is four degrees - that Andres Magallon was required to burn alcohol-soaked pads of cotton wool just to get some heat into the place. The training session consisted of gymnastics and running because we had no balls to practise with."

The Spaniards had been taken to the Liverpool Baseball Association playing fields in Long Lane, Aintree. Across the road was the Lucas factory, which fielded several football teams every weekend. The Echo reported that the team bus driver had located Frank Martin, secretary of the factory's sports committee, who loaned four footballs to the Spaniards. Everton secretary Bill Dickinson later explained that even the Everton players did not train at Goodison and Bellefield was occupied by the Blues. "I believed there would be some official at the LBA ground to provide them with footballs for their training," he told the Echo. "We have had no complaint from the Zaragoza officials at all."

Donate went on: "In this football-mad city nobody dares to come out with comments to the effect that Everton will get through though most people think they will. The atmosphere on the terraces will be more impressive than anything Zaragoza have had to contend with up to now."

Donate pointed out that both clubs were competing in Europe for a fifth season, but Zaragoza had "a much better record". He said that while Everton had played 17 games, won seven and scored 24 goals, the Spanish team had played 37 games, won 23 and scored 80 goals.

The scoreline from the first leg opened up a complex range of possibilities for the evening. A lot would depend on if Zaragoza scored an away goal. Then a 3-1 win on the night to the Blues would result in the Spaniards going though on the away goal rule; similarly so if the score was 4-2 on the night to Everton. However if Everton won the second leg 2-0 to make it 2-2 on aggregate, there would be 30 minutes extra time. If the tie was still deadlocked, a coin would be tossed to decide which team went through. It meant that Everton had to attack to get back into the tie while at the same time trying to guard against a potentially crucial away goal.

Pickering was still out with his knee complaint while Mike Trebilcock seemed to be out of favour. Catterick's centre forward for the evening was Sandy Brown. Although his best position was perhaps full back, he was usually referred to as a utility man. He had played up front in the recent home game against Stoke but he missed several chances and Stoke had won. So it was a bold decision by Catterick.

Brown has gone down in Merseyside folklore as the player who scored an own goal in a derby match with a diving header. But he deserves to be remembered for far more than that. First and foremost, he was a great club servant, making more than 250 appearances. That he played in a wide variety of positions, including emergency goalkeeper, was testimony to his all-round sporting ability and athleticism.

Labone said: "You see those Superstars contests on the TV where different sportsmen compete in endurance tests, Sandy would have won every one. He was very wiry and as strong as a horse. He could walk a mile on his hands. I remember once we went to Tel Aviv for a friendly. We were in a hotel and we bet him that he couldn't swim from one end of the swimming pool to the other and keep a lighted candle alight. Well there's Sandy doing the one-armed breaststroke, holding this candle and we're all standing on the side pelting him with paper cups, anything we can get our hands on. He did it though."

The 56,000 Evertonians that turned up that evening were to see a pulsating game that was broadcast on Spanish radio. Morrissey was ruled out with a hamstring injury while Zaragoza were without Lapetra due to a migraine attack and was replaced by the experienced Isasi who had not played for six months. The Everton team was: West, Wright, Wilson, Gabriel, Labone, Harvey, Scott, Ball, Young, Brown, Temple.

It was to be one of the great European nights at Goodison. In his match report, Donate wrote: "I wish the fans of Real Zaragoza could see how their team play on English grounds ... they defended stoutly and produced some spectacular attacking play of their own. I would also particularly like them to see and hear a crowd of at least 50,000 shouting on the opposition at Goodison Park, to a much greater extent than any match we have seen before at a British ground, and we have seen a few of those in our time ... The booing that greeted Zaragoza's arrival on the pitch will have scared away the wading birds that nest in these parts."

Everton went on the attack from the outset but the Zaragoza defenders showed that they could be just as good as their more illustrious forwards. Scott and Temple hit shots straight at the goalkeeper Yarza while Brown apparently fired in shots whenever he glimpsed goal. Colin Harvey and Gabriel, as usual, worked their socks off in midfield, moving forward whenever they could to support the forwards. The Blues also had to be on their guard as the Spaniards from time to time would quickly break from their own half, resulting in Villa and Pais sending in shots to keep West on his toes. Then there were times when the Spaniards just took their time. Quick throw-in? No way, Jose.

Donate told his readers: "Every Everton player had a Zaragoza player right at his side. You'd have to ask Isasi, Gonzalez and Reija, to name only three, how much ground was covered by Ball, Brown and Scott over 90 minutes. And you'd also have to ask every one of our players to show you the physical marks they picked up as a memory of this match which was tough, as you'd expect against English opposition without being really dirty, although it stretched the limits at times."

The second half saw Everton work even more furiously to try and unpick the Spanish defence. But as the clock ticked away, they increasingly resorted to launching the ball high in the hope of picking up a knock-down. But the centre-half Santamaria was having a fine game, revelling in the opportunity to show his heading ability. The crowd was roaring Everton on. Then with 10 minutes left, Ball pumped up another high ball, Gabriel flicked it downwards and Brown pounced to whack it into the top of the net; Goodison erupted. It was a marvellous moment for Brown who had had a fine game.

The Spaniards knew they had to survive 10 minutes in a floodlit cauldron. From the kick-off, they sent the ball back to the keeper who then dillied and dallied. The crowd bayed at him, Yarza still clutched the ball in his hands so Gabriel shoulder-charged him. Free kick to the Spaniards but Yarza's next bit of time-wasting was so heinous he had a free kick given against him. It was indirect, in the penalty box. It resulted in a furious scramble. Der ball ist rund, but it wouldn't go in the Zaragoza net. Everton were awarded another free kick but the Spaniards held out. Everton won 1-0 on the night but Zaragoza won 2-1 on aggregate.

Donate wrote: "I think those who listened to Matias Prats' radio commentary will appreciate Zaragoza's great defensive display ... and at the final whistle the joy shared by all the players hugging each other and jumping up and down in the centre of the pitch."

The Zaragoza coach Fernando Ducek said: "It might be more spectacular winning the Spanish Cup, but today was more difficult and just wait and see people talking about it all across Europe. I think it's a red letter day for Zaragoza."

The Spaniards were drawn in the next round against Glasgow Rangers. Both legs ended in 2-0 wins for the home team. The Scots went though on the toss of a coin. Rangers then beat Slavia Sofia in the semi-final and faced Bayern Munich in the final in Nuremburg. The game was played the week after Celtic had won the European Cup. After 90 minutes Rangers and Bayern, who included youngsters Franz Beckenbauer and Gerd Muller, were goalless. The Germans won 1-0 in extra time.

Everton's season also ended in disappointment as we failed to qualify for Europe. Over the last five years we had played in all three European competitions and learnt a lot. But Europe now had to do without us. We had finished sixth in the league. The champions were Manchester United. We had enjoyed knocking Liverpool out of the FA Cup in the fifth round with a goal from Ball. But in the quarter-finals we had lost 3-2 to Johnny Carey's Nottingham Forest.

Pickering had finally returned to the team but scored again for Everton in only one more game, a 4-2 win at Aston Villa in May in which he scored twice. But in the reserves Harry Catterick had a promising young No.9, Joe Royle, and Pickering was sold to Birmingham for £50,000 in August 1967. He had scored 70 goals in 115 games for Everton. Big Fred had played nine games in Europe, scoring six goals, all in 1964-65, two in Oslo, two against Kilmarnock and one in each game against United. Forty years later, he was still our top scorer in Europe. Perhaps we need another striker with a quiff.

10. HARE KATTERIK'S HOME GROWN HEROES

Keflavik
European Cup
1970-71

In 1970 Everton were the best team in England. They had won the championship in style, eventually racing away with the title, playing champagne football and winning it by nine points, which was then worth more than four wins. The Blues were so good that half the team were required in Mexico to defend the World Cup for England. Alan Ball, Brian Labone, Tommy Wright and Keith Newton played in the finals. Gordon West was seen as the best reserve for Gordon Banks but told England manager Alf Ramsey he did not want to be away from home for such a long period. There was dismay that Colin Harvey was not selected not least because he could have given the Brazilians some football lessons. Some of us were also disappointed that Howard Kendall was omitted too. Ball, Kendall and Harvey had become such a formidable midfield trio that all the pundits and commentators went into raptures over them. So much so that Labone was to sardonically declare that it was the first time a three-man team had ever won the championship.

A three-year absence in Europe was brought to an end. Everton had finished sixth in 1967, fifth in 1968 and third in 1969. Notably, several of the championship team have stated that they thought Everton played better in 1968-69 than in the following season when we won the championship.

It was infuriating in 1968 when Manchester City pipped Manchester United to the title. We finished fifth and there were four Fairs Cup places for English teams. What's more, both Manchester clubs went in the European Cup because United had won it in May. Did we get in the Fairs Cup? No. The places went to Liverpool who had finished third; Leeds, fourth; Chelsea, sixth; and Newcastle, 10th, who took full advantage of their good fotune and went on to win the Fairs Cup. Ruled out due to the one-club, one-city rule were not only Everton, but the London clubs Spurs and Arsenal.

Of course, we could have gone in the Cup Winners Cup if only we had won the 1968 FA Cup final, but we lost in extra-time to West Brom. Then 1969 was just as infuriating, if not more so, as we finished third in the league and were denied entry to the Fairs Cup only because Liverpool had finished second. It could be argued however that having no European distractions was a blessing in disguise because we won the championship in 1970.

This championship team was remarkable for several reasons: It was possibly the most English team to win the championship and it was probably the most Scouse side ever to win the title. What's more, half the team had come through the club's youth ranks.

If you go through Everton's starting line-ups in the league that season, 90 per cent of players were English, 54 per cent were produced through the youth ranks and 45 per cent were Scousers.

These are figures in which the club and its supporters could take particular pride, certainly if you believe that a football team should have a large degree of representation of players from its home area.

And with more than half the team coming through the youth ranks, it was very cost-effective. It was very John Moores. To explain how I arrived at those figures. There were 42 league games and of course 11 players starting each game, a total of 462 starts through the season.

The players who came through the ranks were: John Hurst, 42 starts, Wright, 42, Royle, 42, Harvey, 35, Labone, 34, Jimmy Husband, 30, Alan Whittle, 15, Roger Kenyon, 8, Gerry Humphries, 1. A grand total of 249, which works out at 54 per cent of 462.

Likewise, to calculate the Scouse percentage, there was Wright, 42, Royle, 42, Harvey, 35, Labone, 34, Whittle, 15, then also Johnny Morrissey, signed from Liverpool reserves who made 41 starts. A total of 209 starts, working out at 45 per cent.

Regards the non-English element, there was that great Scot, Sandy Brown, who made 31 starts, the under-rated Ulsterman Tommy Jackson who - so good he could fill in for Ball, Kendall or Harvey - made 14 starts, and Humphries, from North Wales, with one start. A total of 46, or 10 per cent.

Also it was very much a collection of players who were used to playing alongside each other. With the exception of Newton, who had joined in December 1969, and Jackson, who had joined in 1968, every player had been with the club for at least two full seasons before the start of the glorious 1969-70 season. And even then, the two "newcomers" made just 26 starts between them.

There were other youngsters who broke into the first team in the preceding seasons but were unable to hold down a place. These included Terry Owen and I think I was present at one of his two appearances in April 1968 as I was delighted to see an Owen in the team. I did not realise that we shared the same birthday, September 11. Nor did it cross my mind that he might name one of his sons after me.

The 1969-70 season was a great one for the supporters. There was even a new song for the Gwladys Street to adapt in September 1969 after Radha Krishna Temple went into the Top 20 with the Hare Krishna Mantra, resulting in the chant, a rather quick one, of Hare Katterik, Hare Katterik, Hare Katterik.

After the experience gained from the previous forays into Europe, and the confidence gained from running away with the league, there was considerable optimism about Everton's second entry in the European Cup. Drawing Keflavik brought a mixed response. A trip to Iceland was not an awe-inspiring prospect, but held out great hope of getting into the second round; it was certainly better than playing the best ever Inter Milan team. Nor did we need a tricky tie. Although we were English champions, we had not started the season too well. We failed to win any of our first six games, drawing three and losing three.

Keflavik meanwhile were thrilled to draw Everton and had little hope of going further in the tournament. The club treated the first leg as if it were a holiday break, arranging to spend a few days in London after the game with the 60 supporters who were accompanying them. Coach Holmbert Sigurdsson declared: "We will do our best to keep the score down." The Everton team was: West, Wright, Newton, Kendall, Kenyon, Harvey, Whittle, Ball, Royle, Hurst, Morrissey.

The Everton No.5 shirt had been the preserve of Labone through the Sixties. But injury had forced him to miss the run-in to the title in spring 1970 and the 21-year-old Roger Kenyon had stepped in for the last eight games. Labone had regained his fitness in time for the World Cup finals and had played in the Charity Shield win over Chelsea and in the first three league games of the season. But 500 games for Everton and 26 for England were beginning to take their toll on his body. Kenyon had been drafted in again and enjoyed a run of 16 games while Labone watched from the sidelines.

The game at Goodison turned out to be a tale of two keepers: West and 19-year-old Thorsteinn Olafsson. Although the Icelandic teenager let six goals in, he was the hero of the night. The role of villain was taken by the veteran who had kept goal for his team more than 300 times, pulling off thousands of saves to help the Blues win two championships and a FA Cup. Evertonians like to see themselves as great supporters, but there are times when the behaviour of some is disappointing.

In the 12th minute, Keflavik took the lead with a bizarre goal. West failed to catch the ball and Newton decided to hack the ball clear but his clearance hit the keeper and the ball bobbled into the goal. Still, Everton outclassed the visitors, carving through them time and time again to create chance after chance. It was an ideal opportunity for a goalkeeper to show what he could do and Olafsson pulled off a string of superb saves. This was meant to be the start of the trail to the European Cup final. Losing 1-0 at home to a team from Iceland thanks to a bizarre own goal was not part of the script. Some of the 28,000 crowd became a little restless as the part-timers hung on to their lead. Then the ball was passed back to West who considered his options. He let the ball lie idly on the turf and looked upfield towards the Park End goal. Suddenly he noticed the winger Ragnarsson racing towards him. West dived on the ball in the nick of time, but it was a fright that the crowd did not need. There were angry shouts from some spectators in the Gwladys Street end. In response, West, known as a man who lived on his nerves, gave them the V-sign. His barrackers were incensed and the abuse intensified.

But there was little for the fans to worry about. The game reverted to its expected format. Everton got the equaliser they deserved a few minutes before half time, Ball the scorer. The second-half saw Everton overrun the Icelandic part-timers in the manner the crowd expected. Johnny Morrissey and Jimmy Husband raided down the wings, providing a steady flow of crosses for Royle who scored twice. Olafsson pulled off a series of fine saves but Ball still finished with a hat-trick. Kendall had scored the second of the Blues' six goals. It was 6-1 until Ragnarsson stabbed the ball home after West, who had very little to do in the second half, failed to catch a free kick. It was his last game in European competition for Everton. But the couple of mistakes he made in one game, which did not affect the result, have to be balanced against the blinders he had in Europe, most notably at Old Trafford.

Two days after the game, Catterick announced that he was dropping West. In from the cold came Andy Rankin who had not played in the first team for three years. A local lad, his last appearance had been in May 1967 against Aston Villa. Since then West had played 158 games for the Blues, missing only one game. That was a week before the 1968 FA Cup final when Catterick fielded Geoff Barnett at West Ham in the last away league match of the season. In 1969 Barnett had moved on to Arsenal and played in the 1972 FA Cup final.

Rankin was small for a goalkeeper, but agile and he knew all too well about the wrath of Evertonians. He was always susceptible to jibes due to his moptop hairstyle which seemed to be even longer at the front than at the back. "Get your hair cut Rankin," someone would shout whenever he was thought to be at fault. He was criticised after the 1967 FA Cup quarter-final at Nottingham Forest where he let in three goals as we lost 3-2. It was one of two games for which he is most remembered. At Forest he was the villain, which was perhaps unfair. However, in the other, a European tie, he was to be the hero.

Rankin was to be first-choice keeper for the rest of the season, missing seven games with West deputising on five occasions and Dai Davies twice. However West was to be ever-present the following season.

When Catterick's squad boarded the plane the day before the return leg in Iceland, West was preparing for a reserves match that evening against Manchester United reserves in the first round of the Lancashire Senior Cup. And new on the bookshelves was West's autobiography The Championship In My Keeping. West at least had the consolation of keeping a clean sheet for the Blues' reserves, for whom a youngster called Mick Lyons had an excellent game at centre-half. The only goal came early in the second half from Archie Styles.

Also left behind on Merseyside were Kenyon and Husband. The centre half had needed three stitches in a cut near his eye while the winger was suffering from a hamstring strain. An 18-year-old from the reserves was earmarked for his debut. But winger Gary Jones fell ill as the party travelled to Iceland. On arrival at the team hotel, he was confined to bed with a high temperature. Doctors attributed his illness to the after-effects of a smallpox vaccination he had had two weeks earlier. Also on the plane was 18-year-old goalkeeper Keith Williams who never did make the first team. Meanwhile, Catterick was relieved that after our lack-lustre start to the league season, we had won our last four games to put us back in the top half of the table.

The game was in danger of being postponed following heavy rain. But the local groundsman had an answer. It would seem it was a tried and trusted method in Iceland, but the spreading of lava dust raised eyebrows among the Everton party. There were several pitch inspections but the Northern Ireland referee Malcolm Wright eventually gave permission for the match to go ahead. The Everton team was: Rankin, Wright, K.Newton, Kendall, Labone, Harvey, Whittle, Ball, Royle, Hurst, Morrissey.

The pitch was so muddy that the players at times were slithering and sliding around in front of the capacity crowd of 9,500. Despite the tricky conditions the Blues managed to pass the ball well. Whittle and Morrissey showed their class down the wings, Royle was in a rich vein of form while Harvey was dominating the midfield. Whittle was in the right spot to head home a cross from Morrissey, then Royle had a penalty and scored with a collector's item - a header from a penalty. After Gudnarsson handled in the box, Royle's penalty was pushed out and upwards by Olafsson and big Joe ran forward to nod it into the net. Rankin in the Everton goal was very much a spectator. Everton went in at half-time, 2-0 up. Shortly after the restart, Royle scored with a shot after a cross by Wright. Catterick withdrew Ball and Harvey, sending on substitutes Jackson and Brown. Stay a little bit longer? No, it was 3-0 on the night and 9-2 on aggregate and the game petered out.

Afterwards Catterick appeared to be more relieved at the lack of injuries than pleased with the result. "We could have scored a dozen. We let them off lightly," he said. "But I cannot recollect a more difficult playing surface. There was not only a lot of water on top but also a layer of water under the turf. This made the pitch loose and very difficult for a player to maintain his balance. I was worried before the game that we could have some nasty injuries with players falling and grazing their skin on the lava grit. Fortunately they all came through without injury."

11. BEST GAME I NEVER SAW

Borrusia Monchengladbach
European Cup
1970-71

When Everton drew Borrusia Monchengladbach in the second round, it immediately invoked memories of the dramatic World Cup quarter-final three months earlier in which West Germany had come from behind to knock out England 3-2, especially as the two clubs each had four players out there in Mexico.

The clash of English and German club champions was to be equally dramatic. Monchengladbach had just won the German championship for the first time in the club's 70-year history. And in 1971 they would become the first club to retain the Bundesliga which had been won by seven different clubs. Cologne, Werder Bremen, Munich 1860, Eintracht Braunschweig, Nuremburg and Bayern Munich were the first six; Monchengladbach were the first to win it a second time. By 1977 they had won it five times.

Everton were meeting a club enjoying the start of the greatest chapter in its history. Their best known player was Berti Vogts. He had played in all of Monchengladbach's Bundesliga games since their promotion in 1965 and had been a prominent figure in West Germany's defeat of

England. Midfielders Gunter Netzer, Peter Dietrich and defender Klaus Sieloff had also been in Mexico with West Germany. In addition, winger Herbert Wimmer and defender Ludwig Muller had been capped by West Germany.

Notably too there was the up-and-coming striker Jupp Heynckes who was to play in the national team that won the European Championships in 1972 and the World Cup in 1974. Heynckes was also to have a wonderful managerial career that involved spells at Monchengladbach, Athletic Bilbao, Bayern Munich and Real Madrid. Presumably part of the danger posed by Heynckes the player was not just due to his skill, but also his football brain.

Coach of Monchengladbach in 1970 was Hennes Weisweiler who had been a rugged defender with Cologne. He once suffered a fractured skull early in a game, a promotion decider, and carried on until the final whistle. He had become coach in 1964.

The previous weekend Weisweiler and his captain, Netzer, had travelled to London to see Everton play at Highbury. We lost 4-0 but they both spoke highly of the Blues, saying they would have hoped to have avoided Everton in the early rounds. Weisweiler had earmarked Alan Ball as the man to stop. It also seemed that they were expecting a physical battle. Assistant coach Rudi Schlott said: "We have had a good preparation for this tie because in our last few league games we have come up against some pretty rough teams."

Given the fantastic, flowing football that the Blues played in 1969-70, this seems a little misguided. Perhaps it was something to do with the reputation that British teams in general had on the Continent. Also, the Germans had just seen an Arsenal team that was to win the double that season playing a rather physical, methodical game and no doubt Everton would have tried to stand up to them at Highbury. "We know Everton are a fine footballing team, but they will be hard," said Schlott. Of course, they may also have been aware of the Battle of Nuremburg five years earlier.

Monchengladbach were a wonderful footballing team too and had the nickname "The Colts" which, said some, was due to their willingness to shoot on sight. Perhaps it was for Andy Rankin's benefit that Catterick had the Blues practising at Bellefield with a football said to be of the type used in Germany. Catterick said: "The footballs the Germans use seem to be lighter than the type we use and they tend to swerve and dip."

On the afternoon before the game, the 16-strong squad flew from Speke. On landing in Germany they boarded a coach, which Catterick ordered to go straight to the stadium. It was pouring with rain but Catterick led the players inside for a look around. It had a capacity of 32,000 and was one of those grounds where the crowd was particularly close to the pitch. However, in addition to the travelling Evertonians, around 5,000 British soldiers from the nearby NATO bases were expected to be cheering on the Blues. On the day of the game, the team trained at a British Army sports stadium. It was reported that Catterick had the gates locked to prevent any "spying".

The game had taken on added importance for Everton due to their disappointing league form. The defeat at Arsenal had left the Blues in 13th place and even in September hopes were fading that Everton could retain the title. In a bid to pep the team up, Catterick had gone out and signed Henry Newton from Nottingham Forest. Tommy Jackson had gone the other way in a part-exchange deal, which rated Newton at £150,000. Newton, like Jackson, could play in a variety of positions but it was full-back that he played for England. He also had a reputation as a classy player which wasn't just due to the fact that his hair was always immaculately

Brylcreemed back, although some thought he never quite gelled with the team. Being a recent signing, he was ineligible to play in this second round game.

The first-half was dominated by Monchengladbach who kept Everton pinned back. Netzer was spraying the ball around as if he owned the place. Sure enough the Germans scored the goal they deserved - through Vogts. Everton were 1-0 down at half-time but it could have been worse.

The second half started with a controversial goal. Surprisingly, it was for Everton. It was only a minute or two after the restart and the German goalie Wolfgang Kleff had decided to pick up the toilet rolls that had been thrown on the pitch by Britons when Howard Kendall sent in a shot from outside the box. It flew into the net. The Germans weren't happy. The throwing of toilet rolls had been a familiar, if tiresome, sight in the Sixties at English football grounds, particularly lower league ones. Goalies were frequently seen picking them up, rolling them up a little then tossing them to the back of the goal. In this instance, British squaddies were blamed for the toilet rolls. But surely Kleff should have concentrated fully on the game, instead of being a toilet roll holder.

The equaliser seemed to inspire Everton who came out of their defensive shell to such an extent that Netzer was less influential. The game ebbed and flowed but without further goals. Everton flew home from Cologne Airport happy with the 1-1 draw.

To place that away draw in context, we should fast forward 12 months. Monchengladbach were again at home in the first leg of the second round of the European Cup. The visitors were an Inter Milan team that included four of Italy's 1970 World Cup final team. With Netzer in awesome form, the home team won 7-1. Inter were to win the second leg 4-2. Who should go through? Yes, Inter, who had complained that one of their players had been hit by an empty can thrown from the crowd in the first leg; he was carried off and substituted. UEFA ordered that the first leg should be replayed. The game took place in Berlin and was goalless. In the 1970s, Monchengladbach were in many ways the German Everton.

Monchengladbach had impressed Catterick greatly. Before the second leg at Goodison, a fortnight later, he heaped praise on them, describing the German team as the best he had seen in Europe. It isn't clear whether he meant they were the best at that moment in time, or the best he had ever seen. He may even have been indulging in some "kidology". However it was to be the most enthralling European tie seen at Goodison in Catterick's reign.

The author has watched Everton since 1963 and I look back on this match as the best game I never saw. I went to nearly all the other home games that season but for some reason which I cannot recall I decided to give this one a miss. However I can remember watching the TV highlights that evening, deeply regretting my absence.

It was also a game missed by Brian Labone, albeit only in the playing sense. The 500-plus games he had played for club and country were beginning to take their toll on his body. Injuries were not so easily brushed aside any more and there was the strapping young Roger Kenyon eager to become a regular in the first team. But Labone, who only a few months earlier had been a prominent figure in England's defence of the World Cup, was the ultimate clubman, still keen to help in whatever way he could.

When the German players arrived at Goodison Park and meandered through the narrow corridors they saw the England centre-half pushing a skip. Puzzled that such a great player should be doing such a lowly task, one said to him in English: "Why are you pushing the skip?" "Because I'm not in the team," was the matter-of-fact reply.

It was a game played in pouring rain, but still there was a crowd of around 43,000. If Kleff had been at fault in the first leg, he was to make up for it at Goodison with a tremendous display. He was so good that Catterick went so far as to say he would have given him the Iron Cross. "I have never seen a better goalkeeping display," said the Everton manager. "The lad had a bit of luck at times but he deserved it."

It was another tale of two keepers because Rankin in the Everton goal had the most memorable night of his career, all due to one save. While heaps of praise was lavished on Kleff, the game started with a clanger by him which gave Everton a first-minute lead. Johnny Morrissey put over an innocuous-looking cross which skidded off the wet turf and, evading the grasp of Kleff, skidded into the net.

That goal put Morrissey into the record books as the first Everton player to score in three different European competitions, following his goal in the Fairs Cup at Kilmarnock and one against Aalborg in the Cup Winners Cup. He was to be the only Blues player to record this Euro hat-trick and there cannot be too many players in Europe who achieved that feat.

Despite his mistake, Kleff soon made two breath-taking saves and a double save that had the crowd gasping again. Everton were rampant at times, with Kendall, Morrissey, Colin Harvey and Joe Royle putting in shots that Kleff saved.

In midfield Netzer was pushing though some brilliant balls for Heynkes and Horst Koppel to chase, but the Everton rearguard was coping admirably, so much so that Rankin was rarely troubled. However an equaliser came when Herbert Laumann put in a header that Rankin did well to save. But he could not hold the ball and Laumann pounced to poke the ball home.

The game went to extra time and Catterick made two substitutions, with Sandy Brown replacing Keith Newton and Jimmy Husband coming on for Alan Whittle. Throughout the first 90 minutes there had been an absorbing battle in midfield and that continued for the next half-hour. Kendall was having a magnificent game, putting in those trademark sliding tackles of his. Seemingly all in one motion, he would slide in for the ball, the opponent would tumble over, Kendall would rise to a standing position, looking around at the same time for a spare blue shirt.

In extra time, each team could have won the game, with Husband forcing a fine save from Kleff, and Koppel heading against the bar. But neither side managed to score. After two hours of scintillating football, the referee blew his whistle and signalled for a penalty shoot-out to commence at the Gwladys Street end.

The first penalty was taken by Royle and saved by Kleff. Then Klaus-Dieter Sieloff put Monchengladbach up 1-0 and Ball levelled the score. Next up was Laumann, scorer of the Monchengladbach goal; with Teutonic inefficiency, he put his penalty wide. The tension was rising with each kick. Morrissey held his nerve and scored; likewise Heynkes. After three penalties each, it was 2-2. Next up was Kendall who slotted his kick home, but Koppel, who played with a toupee, did his duty to make it 3-3.

Each team had one penalty left. Who would be man enough to take Everton's last kick? Miss, in front of 43,000 Evertonians, and you would forever carry the cross of being deemed responsible for Everton going out of the European Cup. Brown walked up to the penalty spot, with all eyes upon him. One can only guess at what was going through his mind but he scored to make it 4-3. It all rested on the veteran defender Ludwig Muller, a former Nuremburg player, who had had a fine game. He hit the ball low and hard, and it was goalbound, but Rankin rocketed to his right and palmed the ball to safety. Goodison delirium.

It was one of the great European nights at Goodison. Evertonians talked about little else the next day. But Catterick had other things on his mind. Before the following league game, the normally tight-lipped boss opened up a little, revealng that Ball had been strugging with a groin strain. He added: "Since the World Cup, Ball has been feeling just a little less than 100 per cent. It is a question of too much football in his case."

It appeared that Catterick was rather concerned that the World Cup had taken an exacting toll on Ball, but in the rest of the season he only missed two games. Halfway through the following season, Ball was sold to Arsenal for £220,000. When Ball asked Catterick why he was being sold, the manager told him it was good business; the club had doubled its money. The author sometimes wonders if it had anything to do with the bill for the construction of the new Goodison Road stand, usually referred to as the Main Stand, said to have cost £1million; perhaps not.

Netzer left Monchengladbach in 1973 to join Real Madrid, but only after scoring the winner in his last match for the club, a 2-1 win over Cologne in the German Cup final. This could only have been days after Monchengladbach completed their two-legged UEFA Cup final against Liverpool. Netzer's team won in Germany 2-0 but they had lost 3-0 at Anfield, with Heynckes missing a penalty. See what I mean about the German Everton.

12. CHRISTMAS IN URUGUAY

Panathinaikos
European Cup
1970-71

When the draw for the quarter-finals was made, it was generally thought that Everton had the easiest opponents in the last eight. But Catterick thought differently. He warned before the first leg at Goodison that Panathinaikos were a "much under-rated team" as they possessed a high degree of skill and were physically strong. Their sweeper Aristidis Camaras was described as the top defender in Greek football, with 28 caps to boot. But it was their captain Dimitri Domazos, a midfielder, who was said to be their best player. Up front they had a tall, rangy striker Antonia Antoniadis who, at 24 years of age, was on his way to becoming a legend in Greek football. Already a legend among legends was the Greeks' coach, Ferenc Puskas, who had enjoyed possibly the most remarkable playing career in the history of the game.

He played for only two clubs in a 23-year career, Honved and Real Madrid, and each was widely considered to be the best club side in the world when he was playing for them. He scored more than 250 goals for each team and netted 83 times in 84 games for Hungary until 1956 when Soviet troops crushed an uprising on the streets of Hungary; some of the strongest resistance they faced was said to be from Ferencvaros football fans. At the time Honved were in Austria and Puskas refused to return home. Following political pressure, he ended up with an 18-month ban from FIFA. In 1958, aged 30 and two stone overweight, he joined Real Madrid and went on to win a string of Spanish titles and European Cups, scoring 35 goals in 37 games in European competition for Real.

The brilliant book Puskas on Puskas, edited by Rogan Taylor and Klara Jamrich, tells how Puskas was fairly familiar with the city of Liverpool. Visiting Goodison in 1966 to watch Hungary in the World Cup finals was not his first trip to the city. Apparently he had friends in the North West whom he visited and they would take him to games in Merseyside and Manchester. "Liverpool is a special place, both for its football teams and facilities and also for the great river views from the hill near Everton, with those huge docks all along the bank," he said in the book.

Puskas had played on Merseyside, but not at Goodison or Anfield. It was in front of a capacity crowd however, at Holly Park in Garston, the home of former Northern Premier League club South Liverpool, now the site of the Allerton rail interchange. The game, in May 1967, was a fund-raising event for a community centre.

His visits might have left him thinking that it would be beneficial if his players had a few days' acclimatisation in Liverpool. Although the game was on a Tuesday, he had his squad in Liverpool in time to see the Blues' FA Cup tie at Goodison against Colchester on the preceding Saturday. Howard Kendall and Colin Harvey were in brilliant form but Alan Ball was considered to be below par. Jimmy Husband was outstanding as Everton won 5-0.

The Greeks were staying in Liverpool city centre and it had been arranged that they would train at Southport. Even with subsequent road improvements, the journey today can easily take three-quarters of an hour. Apparently the Greek squad was not too happy with the travelling time involved. Who should come to their rescue? None other than Bill Shankly who said the Greeks could train at his club's Melwood training ground, just three miles from the city centre. Thanks Shanks. It emerged that he was a huge fan of Puskas.

Catterick's gameplan centred around Joe Royle. The Everton boss had concluded that the Greek defence was vulnerable in the air. He wanted the wingers Husband and Johnny Morrissey to fire over as many crosses as possible. Apparently, he also wanted the midfield to lob balls up to Big Joe whenever they saw fit. Puskas also felt that Royle was a threat to his defence which was lacking in six-footers. So he drafted in a reserve, Georgios Kapsis. It was a tall order.

Everton were in only 10th place in the league and with just 11 games left, it looked very unlikely that we would catch the top three of Leeds, Arsenal and Chelsea. Still, we were confident of beating the Greeks by several goals. The team was: Rankin, Wright, K.Newton, Kendall, Kenyon, Harvey, Husband, Ball, Royle, Hurst, Morrissey.

The Greeks gave a dismal display of fouling - tripping, shirt-pulling, obstructing, pushing, kicking - well, that's how it seemed to my 14-year-old football brain. Husband had been in brilliant form in recent games and it appeared that he was marked out for special treatment. As soon as he got the ball, there was two men on him and a third covering. One blow to the knee put him out of the game - after only seven minutes. On came 19-year-old David Johnson who had only played a handful of games. He had managed to score however in his first league game, his FA Cup debut and his first "derby" match. But the youngster was more an inside forward than a winger.

It was to be one of the most frustrating nights in the history of the club. Beat the Greeks and then there was just the semi. The final that year was to be held at Wembley which would probably involve Ajax Amsterdam who had a great team that included Johann Cruyff. What a trip that would be, especially if we returned to the banks of the Royle Blue Mersey as only the second English team to win the European Cup.

Everton had the lion's share of possession against Panathinaikos but simply could not put the ball in the net although we hit the woodwork three times and got three efforts as far as the Greek goalline only for the ball to be cleared at the last moment.

The miserly nature of the Panathinaikos performance seemed so much at odds with the reputation Puskas had as one of the world's most delightful footballers. He deployed just one man up front, Antoniadis, who was powerful in the air and with good ball control for a big man. But he lacked the support to make much headway against Kenyon and Hurst who had few other attacking players to deal with. Andy Rankin did not have a shot to save until midway through the second half. By then the crowd was probably splitting in two between those who thought it was only a matter of time before we scored two or three and those who were beginning to worry about whether we would ever score. Royle was being provided with a steady stream of crosses, but he put three over the bar, one wide and saw another effort kicked off the line. Ball hit the bar from a free kick and Johnson hit the woodwork too. Ball, Kendall and Tommy Wright also missed decent chances.

Then eight minutes from time, the Greeks were given a free kick on the halfway line. Of course, it was played up in the air to Antoniadis. He headed the ball out to Grammos who had sporadically supported him in attack. The wing man passed the ball back and Antoniadis turned and shot into the Park End goal.

The contingent of Greek fans, probably several hundred, went ballistic. The mood among Evertonians was one of deep indignation. The crowd got its voice back and roared the Blues on. Just as it looked as if the Greeks were going home with a most undeserved victory, Royle headed down Everton's 17th corner of the game. Yet another scramble was about to ensue in their goalmouth but Johnson, famed for his speed, got to the ball first and stabbed it home. The goal celebrations were tinged with both relief and disappointment. We were supposed to be going over to Athens with a two or three-goal lead. Instead, it was 1-1.

Panathinaikos were booed off the pitch but Puskas was unrepentant afterwards. "We came to defend," he said candidly. "It was all we could do against a team like Everton on their own ground." Interestingly, he added: "I thought Everton played rather nervously, particularly in the second half because the crowd expected them to score a lot of goals after scoring five last Saturday."

Catterick was philosophical. "We played all the football. We created sufficient chances to have won easily but we didn't stick them in the net. We hit the bar three times and had three efforts kicked off the line."

He added: "The Greeks played no harder than I expected them to. But they will have to play more football than they did tonight."

In the fortnight before the return leg, the Blues had three league games in the space of eight days. On the Saturday there was a 2-0 home win over Stoke, then a midweek trip to Newcastle in which young Welsh keeper Dai Davies made his debut in a 2-1 defeat. This was followed by a 3-2 defeat on the following Saturday at Nottingham Forest. The Liverpool Echo was also giving plenty of coverage to the local schoolboy teams. It carried pen pictures of the Huyton Schoolboys team which had an English Trophy semi-final against Barking. One referred to the No.4, a lad called Peter Reid. "At 5ft 4ins he is the smallest member of the side but that does not stop him getting through a tremendous amount of work in midfield. An Alun Evans fan."

Despite the two league defeats, Everton set off for Athens confident of success. It was decided that the Blues' stay in Athens would be brief - just one night in the Greek capital. This decision was presumably taken after reflecting on a trip the club had made to Athens five years earlier for a friendly. So, on the Tuesday, the 18-man squad had a brief training session at Bellefield then they were driven to the airport for their flight. The game was an afternoon kick-off on Wednesday. Straight after the match they would fly home. It was to be a problematic 24 hours.

When the Everton party finally got to their hotel, they found police patrolling its grounds. This was to stop Panathinaikos supporters from entering the hotel. But until the early hours, Greek supporters drove around in cars and on motorbikes tooting their horns. Others paraded outside the hotel, singing, chanting and whistling. Welcome to Greece. At their hotel they received a visit from a man who told them to expect a torrid time. It was former Everton player, Billy Bingham. He had been manager of Northern Ireland and was to soon take over as coach of the Greek national side. Ten years earlier he had played for Northern Ireland in a World Cup qualifier in Athens which Greece won 2-1.

If the game was to end up in another 1-1 draw, extra time would be played. If that did not lead to a winner, a third game would be held in Milan eight days later. With the game being an afternoon kick-off in springtime Athens, the game was played in a temperature of around 60 degrees Fahrenheit; not too unpleasant. The stadium was not a large one - it had a capacity of 23,000 - but it was full. Some of the Panathinaikos supporters had been in the stadium five hours before kick-off and had steadily worked themselves into a frenzy. "It was like a volcano," recalled Labone. "Billy Bingham came over to our hotel before the game to give us some indication of what to expect. But no-one could have got you ready for something like that. The only light moment came when I spotted a mate of mine in the crowd, in with all the Everton fans behind the fence. Panathinaikos had just got a corner and I suddenly spotted him behind the goal, about three or four seats back. He waved and I winked back."

In the crowd was 12-year-old Steve Parker, from Kensington. He recalled: "I went with my grandad, John Joyce from Kirkby, who was a crazy Evertonian. I was so excited because I was going on a plane, it was my first ever flight. We arrived the night before the game and stayed in a hotel. On the Wednesday afternoon we got a coach to the ground. I can't remember too much about the game. What sticks out in my mind was all the green and white, an awful lot of flags, and it was very noisy."

Husband and Henry Newton had been declared unfit. The team was: Rankin, Wright, K. Newton, Kendall, Labone, Harvey, Whittle, Ball, Royle, Hurst. Morrissey. There was a lively start to the game with the Greeks forcing two corners. But then Everton broke away and Morrissey put over a powerful cross. Royle managed to get his head to the ball but it lacked the necessary direction and skyed over the bar.

If the Greeks were niggly at Goodison, they were blatant at home. The fouls were supplemented by spitting in faces and even eye-gouging. The attitude of the French referee Robert Helies was one of astounding leniency. Or, to use the words of the Sunday Times journalist Brian Glanville, he "outrageously favoured" the Greek team. Morrissey was coming in for some crude attention from the right back Tomaros. At one point both Morrissey and Royle needed attention but the referee refused to let the trainer on. But both got back up and just before half-time Royle nearly scored in two goalmouth scrambles. Der ball ist rund.

The second half started with Panathinaikos on the offensive, in both senses of the word. Domazos went on a great run before slipping the ball to Grommas who crossed for Athanasopoulos, but he dallied and Labone kicked the ball clear. Apparently this so upset Athanasopoulos that he went to punch Labone, but the Everton skipper evaded the flailing arm. Up front, Royle again went close to scoring when the goalie failed to hold on to a free kick by Harvey and the ball fell to Big Joe, but his shot was cleared off the line by Vlahos. Everton claims for penalties were waved away. The game ended 0-0. We were out on the away goals rule.

After the game, Catterick said: "They were spitting in our faces and gouging at our eyes. I thought our players behaved themselves very well under terrible conditions. Under normal circumstances that goalless draw would have been a good result for us. It was the bad result at Goodison that beat us. We should have won the tie there."

Labone recalled: "We should have won, we played superbly over there and should have had a couple of penalties. Alan Whittle was shot down. They were dirty so-and-sos and the refereeing was poor."

Evertonians were gutted, but imagine the feeling if we had known it would be another 34 years before the Blues played in the European Cup again, or its successor, the Champions League. So it is very little consolation that the Greek triumph was a surprise to their manager. In the book, Puskas on Puskas, he said: "I honestly didn't think we'd stand much of a chance against the English champions. I told the players to just relax and play; try to help one another all the time. I didn't give them any fancy tactical instructions; you can draw a lot of pictures on the board, but have you got the players to do it with? Anyway, we drew 1-1 at Goodison and held them to 0-0 at home to go through on the away goal"

Everton flew home straight after the game, landing in Manchester late on the Wednesday night. They then headed to a country hotel to prepare for Saturday's FA Cup semi-final at Old Trafford against Liverpool. Ball, Royle, Harvey and Morrissey were all carrying injuries. Against Liverpool, Ball put Everton ahead after 10 minutes. A few minutes after the interval, Labone went off injured. Liverpool scored twice to win 2-1 with goals from Brian Hall and ruddy Alun Evans. At least the Huyton No.4 would be happy. But young Parker wasn't. He said: "I can remember being so gutted after the Liverpool game. Getting beat by Panathinaikos did not compare to getting beat by Liverpool. The FA Cup meant a lot more to me than the European Cup at that time."

It must rank as one of the bleakest weeks ever for an Evertonian. In just four days, our hopes of progressing to the European Cup final had been crudely shattered and we had lost an FA Cup semi-final to Liverpool - and my adolescent acne was getting worse. I wouldn't have minded the latter so much but it was red.

Some salvation was to be provided by a long-haired Cockney. In May, in school playgrounds and on street corners across Merseyside, Evertonians were scoring goals then lying down on the floor, arms outstretched, in imitation of the Charlie George celebration in the FA Cup final after his winner for Arsenal.

A few weeks later, Panathinaikos were at Wembley, playing Ajax in the European Cup final. The Greeks had overcome Red Star Belgrade in the semis even though they had lost the first leg 4-1. Greece was run by a military junta at the time and after the heavy defeat in Yugoslavia, the officer in charge of the Sports Ministry ordered that the second leg be played at the larger Olympiakos stadium. It was packed out for the game, producing, in the words of Puskas, "a fantastic, frenzied atmosphere". Panathinaikos won 3-0 with two goals from Antoniadis and went through again on the away goals rule. Antoniadis was top scorer in the competition that season, with 10 goals.

The Wembley final was a dismal game, with Panathinaikos playing as if they thought they could even win this on away goals. The Dutch won 2-0. If only the Blue boys could have been there. Even if we had lost to Cruyff's team, there was still a trip to South America because Ajax turned down their invitation to take part in the world club championship. This event between the champions of Europe and South America had been marred by violence on the pitch in previous years. Panathinaikos went in place of Ajax and on December 29 played Nacional in the Uruguyan capital Montevideo. It should have been us.

It had been the sixth time Everton had sent a talented team into Europe and failed to reach the semi-finals. Why had Everton not done better? A good man to ask is Labone, not only because he had played in most of those games, but also he had played for England in mainland Europe and South America. He said: "Perhaps we were not quite good enough or tactically aware enough. I do not think English football generally was up to the tactical expertise of the Europeans. I think they were much more ahead of us, certainly in the 60s, although towards the end of the sixties we became more aware. Also Everton came up against some good sides at the wrong time, Inter Milan, Zaragoza, Ujpest."

Before 1968 only two English teams had won a European trophy. The Cup Winners Cup was won by Spurs in 1963 and West Ham in 1965. It was in the last few years of the Sixties that English clubs began to do better. In 1968, Manchester United, blessed with the exceptional skills of George Best, won the European Cup while Don Revie's tightly organised Leeds won the Fairs Cup. In 1969 Newcastle won the Fairs Cup, possibly using up all the luck that eluded them in the following three decades. In 1970 Manchester City won the Cup Winners Cup and Arsenal won the Fairs Cup. If Everton could have won the European Cup in 1971, it would have been an English treble as Chelsea won the Cup Winners Cup and Arsenal won the Fairs Cup.

Catterick ceased to be team manager in April 1973, just a few weeks before Liverpool lifted their first European trophy, at their ninth time of trying. The Fairs Cup had just been renamed the UEFA Cup and Liverpool were its first winners, beating six clubs over two legs, including four German sides - a fine achievement, it has to be said. It would have delighted Shankly who was to remain manager for just one more season.

Although Catterick and Shankly were opposites, in that one was an introvert and the other an extrovert, there were many similarities in their managerial records. Both men had 12 seasons on Merseyside managing in Division One: Catterick 1961-73; Shankly, 1962-74. Both had masterminded promotions to the top flight, Catterick with Sheffield Wednesday in 1960 and Shankly with Liverpool in 1962. The "Catt" won the league championship twice and FA Cup once. "Shanks" won the league championship three times and the FA Cup twice. Shankly had the edge in terms of trophies, but many Evertonians would strongly argue that we played the more attractive football up until 1971.

Catterick's Everton merited a European place on eight occasions, a great record, although we were barred twice due to the Fairs Cup one-club, one-city rule. Shankly's Liverpool qualified for Europe in ten successive seasons. The Reds were more consistent, sometimes being likened to a machine. The Blues were more cavalier.

Both men were highly respected by their managerial peers. Yet whenever national media pundits write of the managerial greats of the 1960s, the name of Catterick is often left off the list, increasingly so the more time passes by. Shankly would be delighted that he is revered and celebrated in the media so much today, but I suspect he would be surprised and disappointed at the way his arch-rival has been largely forgotten by non-Evertonians. Surely time for a Harry Catterick statue, or even a bust, which could easily be located behind the Park End stand.

13. CANCEL THE VICTORY ROLL

AC Milan
UEFA Cup
1975-76

IT was one of the most infuriating games in Everton history, but the trip to AC Milan ranks as one of the best away trips that Blues supporter George Orr ever embarked upon in his 50 years of following the Blues. "Everything about the performance in Milan was brilliant, Gary Jones was fantastic, the Everton support was great, the whole occasion was just brilliant," he recalled. But Evertonians had needed a good outing after the often bewildering events of 1975.

The 1974-75 season was one in which Evertonians thought we were going to win the championship. From the middle of January until the first week of April we were nearly always top of the table. But we won only one of our last five games and the title went to Brian Clough's Derby County who finished three points ahead of us. We only had ourselves to blame, dropping four points when we lost home and away to newly promoted Carlisle United who finished bottom of the table. And after unexpectedly losing our last home match of the season 3-2 to Sheffield United, we finished in fourth place, one point behind Liverpool and Ipswich. Not only had we blown the title, we had also chucked away the chance to play in Europe. Again, we were left fuming by the one-club, one-city rule. Fifth-placed Stoke would take our place.

There was a fear that Everton were in danger of being left behind. Since 1966-67, we had only played in Europe in one out of eight seasons. In that period, Manchester United, Manchester City, Chelsea, Leeds, Arsenal, Newcastle, Wolves, Tottenham and Liverpool had all reached European finals. In 1973, we had entered the Texaco Cup, an Anglo-Scots affair, as some kind of consolatory effort, but we went out of that at the first hurdle, to Hearts, by one goal of course. Such was the desire at Goodison to get back into Europe that the club decided to appeal against the one-club, one-city ruling. After all, the Inter-Cities Cup had been renamed the UEFA Cup. Surely, clubs should be in purely on merit, Everton argued in Geneva, and the one-club, one-city rule was nothing more than an historical anomaly. Everton won the appeal. The rule change was to take effect immediately, putting us in the draw for the forthcoming tournament, at the expense of Stoke who understandably were very unhappy. They believed that the rule-change should have taken effect the following season. After all, we knew what the rules were when we kicked off the 1974-75 season and Stoke had finished that season celebrating a place in Europe. It was cruel on them.

Billy Bingham, aged 44, became the second manager to take Everton into Europe. Born in Belfast, he had first joined Everton in 1960 as a 29-year-old right winger, and scored 26 goals in 98 games for the Blues before losing his place midway through the 1962-63 season to Alex Scott. Subsequently Bingham moved on to Port Vale. After hanging up his boots - or putting them in a box in the shed - Bingham made a name for himself as an astute manager, with Southport, Plymouth, Linfield, then internationally with Northern Ireland and Greece.

Many Evertonians felt that Bingham's teams did not play with the same flair as the Catterick sides. But football was entering a new era in which more thought was given to countering the opposition. Bingham's boys were a formidable force and certainly capable of knocking the ball about. Indeed, possession football was a term used by critics to describe their style of play. Of course, no Blues wanted to see them give the ball away to the opposition, but they wanted the team to be less adverse to risk. Bingham had to deal with a deep sense of frustration felt by Evertonians who had expected the Blues to sweep all before them in the early Seventies.

The years 1972-74 were a tough time for Evertonians of my age. School discos and similar events would often end with the disc jockey putting on You'll Never Walk Alone. I wasn't the only contrary-minded Evertonian who did just that - walked home alone. It is still incomprehensible how virtually all the girls on the dancefloor would put their arms in the air and start bawling out the words, or the four they knew. You could have spent the last half-hour nervously and rather woodenly dancing with a girl, asking her often if she came here often, then just when you thought you were making progress, the disc jockey would put that record on. It was better just to walk off, because trying to take the DJ's plug out of the wall could lead to a lot of trouble. Likewise turning the lights on as you left the hall.

I asked an Evertonian friend who grew up in a different part of Merseyside in the same era if that recollection struck a chord with him, and if he now found it all wryly amusing. He replied: "I was there too - far too vivid a memory to be funny; quite sad really."

But we had our red letter days too. There was that "JFK moment", still being able to remember today exactly where I was when I heard that Bill Shankly was quitting Liverpool - working on a farm in Birkenhead, or its outskirts. The Koppites were gutted. I was so delighted, especially when I heard that he was being replaced by that fella with the flat cap. But Bob Paisley was a genius.

In Bingham's first full season in charge, 1973-74, Everton finished seventh and made early exits from the domestic cup competitions but he bought the Birmingham scoring sensation Bob Latchford in a deal which saw Howard Kendall and full-back Archie Styles go to St Andrews. The following season, Latchford scored 17 league goals as we finished fourth, subsequently qualifying for Europe.

On the Saturday before the home leg against Milan, Everton had a 3-0 win over a Newcastle team managed by Gordon Lee. The Milan squad, after arriving in Liverpool, had a training session at Runcorn FC's Canal Street ground. It was possibly as they gazed in awe at the Runcorn-Widnes Bridge, remarking at its similarity to the Sydney Harbour Bridge, that they heard the dramatic news from home. A takeover bid had been launched by Gianni Rivera, the former pin-up boy of Italian football who had played for AC for 15 years. It was thought that if he succeeded, the coach Gustavo Giagnoni would be on his way. It didn't help the coach's case that he described Rivera as a "capricious child".

AC Milan had enjoyed glorious spells in the 1950s and 60s. It was kick-started by their plundering of the Sweden team that had won Olympic gold in 1948, signing Gunnar Gren, Gunnar Nordahl and Nils Liedholm, who became known as the GreNoLi trio. Gren and Liedholm played in midfield, feeding Nordahl upfront who scored 210 goals in 257 matches. AC Milan's championship success in 1951 was their first since 1907. They won the title a further three times in the Fifties, taking their total of Scudettos to seven.

The Sixties were even better for Milan. After another Scudetto in 1962, they became the first Italian club to win the European Cup, beating Benfica at Wembley in May 1963, with a man-of-the-match display from Rivera and two goals from Brazilian striker Jose Altafini.

Spookily, in 1968, just like Everton in 1985, Milan were league champions, finished runners-up in the national cup competition and won the Cup Winners Cup in Rotterdam. The following season they entered the European Cup and reached the final in May 1969, beating Ajax Amsterdam. As if that was not enough, they beat Estudiantes to win the world club championship and Rivera won the European Footballer of the Year award.

The 1970s hadn't started badly either. There were more Italian Cup successes in 1972 and 1973 when, managed by Liedholm, they won the Cup Winners Cup again. So Everton were up against a club well versed in the arts and wily ways of European competition.

Bingham pointed out to reporters that Everton had started the season by scoring in all eight games, but warned that the Blues would have to be patient against Milan. Through the Liverpool Echo, he told Evertonians he did not want them "to pressurise the players into stampeding up front". The Everton team he sent out was: Lawson, Bernard, Seargeant, Pearson, Kenyon, Lyons, Buckley, Dobson, Latchford, Smallman, Jones.

Notably, there were only 32,000 fans at Goodison. There was delight when Bob Latchford put the ball in the net on 14 minutes but the Belgian referee Alfred Delcourt blew for a foul. It didn't matter, we thought, there was plenty of time left. But we managed to create precious few other chances in the first half. Partnering Big Bob up front was David Smallman, signed from Wrexham six months earlier for £75,000. He was not quite 6ft tall and was of spindly build, but his touch was exquisite and he was adept at turning defenders to create a yard of room for himself. However the 22-year-old was having little joy against the Milan defenders who were proving masterful spoilers.

Even Gary Jones was finding it hard going. He liked to cut in from the flanks and had been in such a rich vein of form he had prompted comparisons with George Best. A local lad, Jones certainly had the long black hair, the balance, swerve and verve.

The ever elegant Martin Dobson was trying to weave a way through in midfield where he was supported by Mick Buckley, Jim Pearson and Mick Bernard. Buckley was a former England Schoolboys sensation from Manchester who was small and slight but skilful enough to be considered someone out of the Colin Harvey mould. Pearson was a skinny six-footer who favoured the feather hairstyle of the day but he could look after himself, being quite happy to put his foot in where and when necessary. He often played up front, usually to good effect. Bernard, signed from Stoke, was sturdily built and a strong tackler, but surprisingly nimble-footed and skilful enough to win several England caps; he often played at full-back where he would sometimes engage in banter with the crowd.

But as hard as they tried, the Blues could find few ways through the Italian rearguard. The Everton defence also looked secure with Steve Seargeant sweeping behind Mick Lyons and Roger Kenyon - notably all three had come through the club's youth ranks - leaving little to do for goalkeeper David Lawson. As the players trooped down the tunnel at half-time, Evertonians began to wonder if we would ever break down the Milan defence.

Thankfully, when the second half started, the Blues stepped up a gear. Pearson forced a good save from Albertosi, there were penalty appeals by Latchford and Dobson when each felt he was pushed as he went for a header. The 32,000 crowd cranked up the volume although a deep sigh of anxiety could be heard when Aldo Maldera broke clear for the Italians, racing towards the Everton goal but Lawson, who had had very little to do, proved his worth by deflecting the Italian's shot wide for a corner.

Bingham made substitutions, first bringing on Dave Clements for Buckley on the hour. Clements, the dependable Northern Ireland captain, had an unusual gait which led to him being nicknamed "The Crab" as he seemed to run forwards in a sideways manner, but he had far more skill than the mickey-takers gave him credit for. Smallman was substituted too, replaced by John Hurst who went into defence, allowing Lyons to go up front. The aerial bombardment began. Lyons and Latchford were the targets, with Pearson and Dobson weighing in to add their height. It was like the Italian version of The Alamo. But in this Spaghetti Western the good guys didn't win.

A Latchford header whizzed over the bar, Clements powered in a shot that went the wrong side of a post and Big Bob evaded outstretched Italian legs to put in a shot but missed the target. It was so frustrating, and there was more annoyance to come in the last minute when Bernard was sent off after a tangle with the AC captain Romeo Benetti who earlier in the game had, said Bingham, punched Pearson in the back of the head. The Belgian referee had earlier booked four Milan players, including Benetti after a bad foul on Gary Jones, but not Bernard. It seemed harsh to send Bernard off, particularly as it meant he was banned from the return leg.

Before the second leg a fortnight later, Everton had two games at Highbury - drawing 2-2 in the league in front of 25,000, then beating Arsenal 1-0 in a League Cup replay - before a goalless draw with Liverpool at Goodison. Everton flew to Italy with plenty of optimism. If they could score just one goal, the Italians would have to score two, due to the away goals rule. Bingham, due to his spells as a national team manager, had plenty of experience of games on the Continent and knew that surprises may be in store. Dai Davies recalled: "I don't remember anything about the flight or build-up to the game other than in the hotel Billy Bingham telling us not to eat the fruit. He was a bit concerned it might have been tampered with. That might sound strange, but you have to remember it was a different age."

Appointed to referee the game was Rudi Gloeckner, from East Germany, who was rated so highly he had been given the honour of officiating the 1970 World Cup final between Brazil and Italy.

It was to be an evening that tested Gloeckner to the full. Even before the game kicked off, there was controversy. The Milan officials did not want to hand in their teamsheet until Everton had done so. Little did they think that Bingham would have a copy of the UEFA Cup rules handbook in his pocket. Although it said both teamsheets had to be submitted half an hour before kick-off, it stipulated that the home team was under an obligation to hand over their sheet first. Bingham refused to hand over his team list. The UEFA official in the middle of this row must have been at the end of his tether because apparently he talked of postponing the game. Bingham had called on the negotiating skills of John Moores, then the club's vice chairman, and eventually the UEFA official told Milan they would have to submit their teamsheet first. Everton club chairman Alan Waterworth was in Liverpool. The next day's Echo published a photograph, showing him listening to a radio at the Adelphi hotel where he was attending the autumn dinner of the Merseyside branch of the Institute of Directors, of which he was also chairman.

There was a fierce welcome for the Everton team in the San Siro. Davies, who had marbles thrown at him during the game, wrote in his 1986 autobiography Never Say Dai: "The stadium was an odd combination of showground and bullfighting arena. It was impossible to hear fellow players talking or even shouting.

Immediately behind me for the first half, a man was posted behind with a loudspeaker through which he consistently hurled every abuse imaginable from libels about my own mother to the Queen Mother."

The most enthralling player on the pitch in the San Siro that night was Jones, the Scouser who with one shimmy could leave a defender stumbling - ask Tommy Smith of Liverpool. Even the Italians were applauding Jones the footover. But the man who had most impact on the game was the referee, Gloeckner. It is easy to criticise a referee, the man in the middle who has to make a split-second decision relating to the projectile of a ball and the fast and furious movements of opposing players.

Two years later Clive Thomas was to go down in the history of Everton as the referee from hell, inexplicably disallowing Bryan Hamilton's winner against Liverpool in the FA Cup semi-final. Thomas's doubting - that Everton could possibly beat Liverpool for the first time in six years - was captured on TV for all to see. But that was one decision, albeit a horrendous one that haunts Evertonians, and possibly him too, to this day. In Milan in September 1975, Gloeckner made a series of decisions from the first minute to the last that left the Everton players dumbfounded. Bingham, essentially a conservative man, was so angry at the German's decisions that even in the first half he considered taking the team off the field.

In a nutshell, the game hinged on penalty decisions. Midway through the second half the ball struck Lyons' hand. A penalty was awarded and Calloni scored the only goal of the tie. That the ball hit Lyons' hand was not disputed, but he insisted that it was accidental and should have been treated as ball to hand. "The ball bounced up and flicked my hand," he said. Apparently Gloeckner was 30 yards away. Arguably if there was any doubt, he should not have given a penalty. Contrast with Jones' penalty appeal in the first half. He was said to be 10 yards inside the Milan penalty area when Sabadini pulled his shirt. The offence was spotted by Gloeckner who blew his whistle and gave a free kick, outside the area. Bingham said later: "At that moment the utter futility of it all struck me. I felt there was just no way we could win. I felt like calling the team off the field."

A few minutes after the Italian goal, Pearson felt he should have had a penalty after being floored in the box, but Gloeckner didn't see it that way. As Everton went for the equaliser that would have sent them through to the next round on the away goals rule, Buckley was subbed by Darracott and Lyons sent into attack. As Everton piled on the pressure, they went agonisingly close to a goal in the last few minutes. After another run by Jones, the ball fell to George Telfer who sent over a cross which Dobson met with a solid, goalbound header. Albertosi unfortunately pulled off a superb save. The game ended 1-0 to AC.

In fairness to the East German referee, Gloeckner did disallow a "goal" by Giarugu. But the Everton players and managers made damning criticisms of his display. Lyons felt that the referee was determined to give Milan a penalty. Bingham said: "It was obvious that we would have to get a clear-cut goal for it to count."

Of course, this could be interpreted as sour grapes by the Everton party. It is coincidental that the previous season Borussia Monchengladbach were left dumbfounded by some of the Spanish referee's decisions in Germany in the second leg of their Cup Winners Cup semi-final against AC Milan. Two years earlier AC Milan had defeated Leeds in the 1973 Cup Winners Cup final in Salonika in a game in which Leeds had several penalty claims refused by a referee, Christos Michas, who was later suspended.

Orr said: "Everything was against us, but the team were brilliant, especially Gary Jones who even had the Italian fans clapping him. At the end, all the Everton fans stood and applauded the team off. Then we got our coach windows put in, but we just drew the curtains and held them down. It was still a great trip. We came across the team at the airport and Billy Bingham offered to buy all the supporters a drink, which no-one took him up on. We were just so proud of them. I always remember as we walked up the steps of the plane. All the cabin crew were greeting us as we got on and one lad said, 'Is it possible to pass a message to the captain? Well, tell him to cancel the victory roll - we got beat.'"

It was the second time Everton had played a Milan club in European competition. Against AC, just like Inter, the first leg had been a goalless draw at Goodison and the return had been a close affair with the Italians scoring the only goal of the tie in the second half at the San Siro. But this time the Milanese did not go on to win the tournament. After struggling past Athlone in the next round, AC Milan overcame Spartak Moscow before being knocked out by the Belgian club Brugge in the quarter finals. Everton finished 11th in the league and again made early exits from the domestic cups.

In his autobiography, Davies commented on Everton's venture to Italy: "It was an important night for Everton. Though the previous season had been a good one, nothing had been won and the pressure was beginning to increase on Billy Bingham's shoulders. Everton is a club that always expects success and Bingham when he arrived had promised success in Europe. That night I saw once again the strain at the top showing on the face of our manager. It is a terrifying, debilitating strain."

Bingham was later seen with a smile on his face however, guiding Northern Ireland to the World Cup finals in 1982 and 1986.

14. BALLYKISSANGEL AWAY

Finn Harps
UEFA Cup
1978-79

Finn Harps sounded more like a folk music band than a football club. They were based in the little town of Ballybofey in picturesque County Donegal in the north-west of Ireland. It was a relaxing introduction to European football for Everton manager Gordon Lee who had taken over from Billy Bingham a season and a half earlier in January 1977.

Lee, poached from Newcastle, had only been Everton manager for two months and he was leading us out at Wembley in the League Cup final. It was our first game at Wembley for nine years but it was goalless and Aston Villa won the second of 2 replays. Lee took Everton to the FA Cup semi finals that season too, but it was the Clive Thomas game in which the Welsh referee disallowed a perfectly crap goal by Everton. There was nothing illegal about it - the only problem was that it was ungainly, coming off the thigh, or the side, but not the hand, of Bryan Hamilton. We lost the replay.

Only Mick Lyons, Martin Dobson, Bob Latchford, Terry Darracott and George Telfer remained from the Everton team that had travelled to Milan just three years earlier. After defeat in the San Siro, Bingham's Blues had finished the season 11th in the league. It was halfway through the following season, in January 1977, that Bingham was sacked. The timing was surprising. We were in the semi-finals of the League Cup, in the 4th round of the FA Cup and Bingham had been allowed a month earlier to fork out £200,000 fees for Duncan McKenzie and Bruce Rioch.

We finished ninth in the table. The passports stayed in the bedside cabinet again. But the following season, Everton came third with 30 league goals from Bob Latchford. We were back in Europe.

As we prepared to cross the Irish Sea in September 1978, Lee was tying up a deal to sign the classy England defender Colin Todd from Derby for £330,000. He had recently brought in that much by selling Duncan McKenzie, Mick Buckley and Jim Pearson. Some of the supporters were not happy, complaining that Lee's style of play was dull and dour.

The team flew on Monday morning from Liverpool to Dublin then endured a long coach journey to the north-west of Ireland and little Ballybofey which, sitting on the River Finn, could easily have doubled as the setting for a BBC TV series from the 1990s, Ballykissangel. The seats in the club's stand had been bought from the local cinema for 50p each. "It was one of those places which seemed to have little more than a pub and a post office," recalled Blues defender Billy Wright, aged 20 at the time.

The Finn Harps club had only been formed in 1954. They first came to prominence in Irish footballing circles in 1968, winning the FAI Junior Cup which inspired them to apply to play with the "big boys" in the League of Ireland.

Given the enthusiasm in Ireland for football, it is perhaps a shame that the country does not have at least one big club, competing in the English league in the way that Wrexham and several other Welsh clubs have done. But the development of football had taken place against the backdrop of the island's turbulent politics and religious differences. Such was the discord that for more than 20 years there were even two different Ireland teams.

Football had taken a foothold in the Belfast area before taking off in the south in the 1880s. Accordingly the Irish Football Association (IFA) was based in Belfast and viewed with some suspicion by the increasing number of clubs that were formed in Dublin. Tension rose after the 1916 Easter Rising in Dublin and the partition of Ireland in 1921 into six counties in the North and 26 counties in the rest of the isle.

It was in June 1921 - after officials insisted that the Irish FA Cup final replay between Shelbourne, from Dublin, and Glenavon, from Ulster, should take place in Belfast, not Dublin - that the Football Association of the Irish Free State (FAIFS) was set up, breaking away from the IFA. The football associations of England, Wales and Scotland blacklisted the FAIFS but in 1923 FIFA accepted the Free State's application. Three years later they played their first international, losing 3-0 to Italy in Turin.

Thus began the bizarre situation where there was two Ireland football teams, one picked by the IFA, the other by the FAIFS. Some Everton players won caps from both associations. Tommy Eglington made 24 appearances for the Republic and six for Northern Ireland while Peter Farrell played 28 times for the Republic and eight times for Northern Ireland. This anomaly was not resolved until 1950 when FIFA told each association to only pick players from within its jurisdiction. Three years later FIFA had to intervene again because both associations were calling their national team Ireland. One was ordered to call itself the Republic of Ireland and the other, Northern Ireland.

History was created at Goodison Park in 1949 when one of these Ireland teams - the one headquartered in Dublin - became the first overseas nation to beat England on their own soil, with Farrell scoring one of the two goals on his home ground in an away match.

It was not until 1969 that Finn Harps were admitted to the League of Ireland (LoI), making them the only "senior" club from County Donegal. After losing their first LoI game 10-2 to Shamrock Rovers, there were fears that Harps were out of their depth. But they went on to enjoy a relatively successful spell in the 1970s, qualifying for Europe four times.

Everton were the fourth club in six seasons to visit Ballybofey for a European tie. Harps had travelled to Turkey in the Cup Winners Cup in 1974, losing 4-2 on aggregate to Buraspor. The year before they had lost to Aberdeen in the UEFA Cup 7-2 over two legs. But there was considerable embarrassment in 1976 when they went out on an aggregate score of 16-1 after Derby hammered them in one game 12-0. But throughout the 1970s, Harps finished in the top half of the LoI table and gained a reputation for attractive football.

The conditions for the visit of Everton were just what underdogs would want. It was pouring down and there were a lot of wet Evertonians but they were soon singing in the rain after the Blues took a two-goal lead within 15 minutes. First Dave Thomas scored then Andy King. Everton continued to knock the ball around, just waiting for the right time to play an incisive pass. Harps' Tony O'Doherty was lively in midfield but this was an area dominated in the main by Trevor Ross who was deputising for the injured Dobson.

Everton scored again after Ross won the ball in midfield with one of his trademark crunching tackles and delivered a great pass for King to beat goalkeeper Eddie Mahon. He had only picked the ball out of the net three times when he went off, Ballykissangel-style, with a bad back to be replaced by substitute keeper Joe Harper for the last half hour. He was beaten, for goals four and five, by Latchford and his striking partner Mick Walsh in a two-minute spell. Straight after the match the Everton party set off on the journey home, touching down at Speke in the early hours.

Meanwhile, John Moores was 81. Some might have thought that he would now be making plans to arrange an orderly handover of his controlling bloc of shares in Everton; in effect, designating his successor. But he had a bigger issue to deal with: training someone in the family to whom he could hand over the reins of the Littlewoods empire he had built up with his brother Cecil.

There were three main parts to the Littlewoods empire: football pools, mail order and the chain of high street shops. Ownership of this huge empire was totally in the hands of the family. The Littlewoods Organisation was later to be described as "Britain's biggest and most secretive private company".

With such an emphasis on keeping the company under the control of the family, one might assume that Moores always hoped that one of his children would take over. He and his wife Ruby, who died in 1965, had two daughters and two sons. The girls were sent to Cheltenham Ladies College and the boys to Eton. Ironically, the Everton boardroom overlooks Eton Street, which runs down to County Road.

The daughters married and brought up families. In 1947, Betty wed a tax lawyer, Kenneth Suenson-Taylor, whose father was made the first Lord Grantchester, and set up home near Wimbledon. Janatha was to marry a man called Patrick Stubbs. Subsequently they would spend a lot of their time in Malta.

The boys both entered the family firm. John junior, born in 1928, started at Littlewoods' Kirkby garage in 1946, cleaning cars and stripping down engines, before becoming manager of the company's Scunthorpe store in 1949. It has been said that he was being groomed to take over, that he went to business school in America then returned to manage the retail arm. But apparently in 1971 after a disagreement with his father over strategy, he quit.

Although John junior was to maintain a strong interest in Littlewoods, he was to spend a lot of time on breeding Aberdeen Angus cattle. I cannot offer an explanation for this, other than to suggest that, like me, he was a fan of the 1960s' TV series Bonanza, about a man and his sons who looked after a cattle ranch called The Ponderosa. John junior also took a keen interest in social issues.

Peter, born in April 1932, also entered the family business. After Eton, he had gone to Oxford to study Italian and German. His great passion was opera and so he had gone to Austria where he was a production assistant with the Vienna State Opera for three years. It was in 1957 that he entered the family business, in the year of his 25th birthday. He was only in his early 30s when he set up the Peter Moores Foundation, a charitable organisation to make donations to the arts and social projects.

In all four children, there had been instilled a strong sense of civic duty, which became evident as they all made contributions in various ways to helping people. However none of them, claimed critics, possessed the same flair for business as their father. That criticism may have been a little harsh. Their father had struck on the right business ideas at the right time and propelled those ventures forward with the help of his brother Cecil. As time went on, however, all three Littlewoods businesses were to face increasing competition no matter who was in charge.

John Moores would also have considered Cecil's sons, Patrick and David, as possible successors. Patrick was said to be a charismatic man, with a penchant for motor car racing. This was something that worried his father who reportedly persuaded him to give up the sport. However fate was cruel. He died in a road accident in the south of France, leaving two children, including Louise, who was mentioned in Chapter 5. It was against a background of tragedy in 1977 that Peter Moores took over as chairman of Littlewoods.

A year later Everton had a new chairman, Philip Carter. He had only been a director at Goodison for two years but he was a trusted lieutenant to Moores, having joined Littlewoods in 1948 and worked his way up the company ladder, becoming in 1976 managing director.

After returning from Ireland, Everton had drawn 1-1 at Villa Park thanks to a goal by Walsh, then the Blues had defeated Wolves 2-0 at Goodison with goals from Latchford and King. We were second in the table after seven games.

The second leg at Goodison was more than anything an occasion for the Finn Harps players to savour. Felix Healy was determined to enjoy himself and ran at the Everton defence whenever he got the ball. The crowd of 21,611 patiently waited for Everton to open the scoring midway through the first half when Andy King curled in a shot from just outside the box. A few minutes later Latchford flicked in a near-post header. It was now 7-0 on aggregate and there was still another hour to play. It would have been nice for the

Donegal team to score and Joe Logan and Paul McGuinness both tested George Wood.

Harps battled gamely as Everton struggled to raise their game above a canter. Everton finally stretched their lead in the 53rd minute when Walsh capitalised on a mistake in the Harps defence. A few minutes later Ross slotted the ball past Harps' Harper for the fourth goal of the night. The goalie then went off with a shoulder injury to be replaced by Mahon. Almost the first thing the substitute did was pick the ball out of the net after a goal by Dobson. It was 5-0 on the evening and 10-0 on aggregate. Remarkably, the last 25 minutes were goalless, which would have at least been a source of consolation for Mahon. It was Harps' last game in Europe for a long time.

15. ALL I WANT FOR CHRISTMAS...

Dukla Prague
UEFA Cup
1978-79

Next was the Czech Army which in 1947 had formed Dukla Prague. The Czech nation had a fine footballing pedigree and by conscripting the country's best players for army service, Dukla Prague became one of the most highly respected teams in Europe. Before the Second World War, football in the Czech capital had been dominated by Sparta Prague and Slavia Prague. The Czechoslovakian league also took in the Bratislava clubs Slovan and Inter. But such was the strength of Dukla Prague that they outclassed all of these, and others, to win the championship eight times between 1953 and 1966, including four times on the trot between 1961 and 1964. They were frequent participants in the International Soccer League tournament in North America. It was during this time that Dukla beat Everton 7-2 in the U.S.

Despite all the club's footballing triumphs, they are best remembered by many as the team immortalised in the early 1980s by the Wirral band Half Man Half Biscuit's record "All I Want For Christmas Is A Dukla Prague Away Kit", which referred to the table football game Subbuteo and the dozens of different-clad teams the enthusiast could collect. Subbuteo did not have a Dukla Prague team at the time this song came out, but later brought out a Dukla home kit.

When Dukla came to Goodison in October 1978 they had just emerged from a barren spell in which they had gone from 1966 to 1977 without winning the Czech championship. However they were on their way to winning the Czech championship again, for the second time in three years. Their star player was Zdenek Nehoda who had helped Czecholslovakia win the 1976 European Championships.

Gordon Lee had sent out reserve team coach Colin Harvey and scout Tommy Jones to Czech to spy on Dukla who were coached by 58-year-old Jaroslav Vejvoda. Dukla arrived in Liverpool on Monday night, 48 hours before the game. They had asked if they could train the next day on Goodison Park, but Everton refused, citing concern for the pitch. Instead Dukla were offered the facilities of Bellefield, where they trained, then went to Goodison to acquaint themselves with the stadium.

The Czechs were expected to defend stoutly and counter-attack through international strikers Miroslav Gajdusek, who had 30 caps to his name, and 26-year-old Nehoda who had more than 50. The latter has gone down in history as one of Dukla's best ever players.

Everton were going well after the first ten games of the league season, lying in second place behind Liverpool. But apparently Mick Lyons felt the need to appeal through the Echo to the fans to get behind the team against Dukla. "Away from home the support has been absolutely tremendous. At home, if things aren't going well, you can hear the groans and it can affect the players a bit. I know that some of them disagree with the way we play but we all want the same end result."

The football produced by Everton in the Sixties was so good that even in 1978 many Evertonians were still harking back to the Catterick teams. Billy Bingham had felt this wrath first. Lee had also arrived at Goodison with a reputation as a manager whose teams played methodical football.

The talk before the game was that Everton needed a two-goal cushion to take to Prague. Preferably that would be a 2-0 scoreline because if the aggregate score was level, then Dukla would have no away goal to count as double. The classy defender Colin Todd was ineligible for the game and so Lee recalled Terry Darracott. The crowd got well behind the team, with a tickertape reception from the Gwladys Street inspired by scenes from that summer's World Cup finals in Argentina.

Mike Pejic recalled: "Dukla were a typical European side of that time, very tight, very hard to break down and counter attacked very quickly. They sat back at Goodison and played a short passing game, passed the ball sharply. In Prague they pushed players forward, opened us up quicker, moved the ball around quicker."

But the Blues got the start they wanted. Latchford scored in the 19th minute after playing a one-two with Martin Dobson, then using his strength to hold off two defenders to put in a neat shot that beat the advancing keeper Karel Stromsik. The 20-year-old Stromsik later pulled off fine saves from Bob Latchford and Dobson as Everton piled on the pressure. Stromsik also got his body in the way of a Trevor Ross powerdrive and the ball slithered away out of danger. Gajdusek was proving a threat to the Everton defence, forcing George Wood to make two good saves. Nehoda however was having a rather quiet game.

Then in the 79th minute Everton got the second goal they so badly needed. Neil Robinson, who had only come on as a substitute for

Terry Darracott a few minutes earlier, put over a cross that King turned home. Goodison erupted and burst into song. Eight minutes later it was struck silent. A free kick on the goalline was whipped in by Nehoda, and the ball fell to Dukla defender Ludek Macela who stabbed the ball home. What made it all the more frustrating was that he had been carried off the pitch injured and it looked as if he was to be substituted. But he strode back on to be a Goodison killjoy to make it only 2-1 to Everton.

After the game Lee said the freekick had been an unnecessary one to concede. Wood said of Nehoda's cross: "We didn't react quickly enough and that was it."

Seventeen years later Pejic recalled: "I gave the free kick away. Gordon Lee gave me a right rollocking when we got in the dressing room. I said, 'Well, couldn't we have defended the kick better?' We defended too deep on top of the keeper."

Lee, with the away goals rule in mind, said: "They were dead and would have had to beat us 3-0. Now they only have to beat us 1-0 because we gave a stupid goal away."

Consequently when Everton flew out to Prague, Lee was emphasising the importance of Everton scoring an away goal themselves. It was all he wanted for Christmas. The players were in buoyant mood. Three days earlier the Blue had defeated Liverpool for the first time in seven years, thanks to a glorious goal from Andy King. Lee took a squad of 16 plus Lyons and David Jones who were both recovering from injury but keen to go on the trip with the rest of the players.

Lee was cautiously optimistic. "Saturday's result was a tremendous boost but we have got to apply ourselves again. I want to treat this as much like a normal away game as possible. Whether that will be possible in a strange country with an unfamiliar ground and different refeeeing interpretations I don't know. But we have done well away from home and we know we can score goals in away games."

Pejic said: "We were quite a competitive side, and with the likes of Dave Thomas and Andy King we had very good technical players. We were more than a match for anyone."

There was optimism too among the travelling supporters who included Donny MacKechnie, from the Scotland Road area of Liverpool. He said: "There were about six or seven of us who went by train. It took us two days but before that we had to spend a day going to London and back to get a visa from the Czech Embassy. There was quite a few Evertonians in Prague although I could not put a figure on it."

It would not have been surprising if any of the travelling Evertonians had claimed political asylum. Liverpool had won the European Cup in two successive seasons and their supporters were insufferable. I have an admission to make here to my friends in the Everton fundamentalist movement: I supported Liverpool on the night of their first European Cup final when they beat the German Everton. My dad had warned me about my behaviour that evening in 1977 as we sat in front of the television and he was right. But some of my mates had travelled to Rome on those special trains from Lime Street and I thought it was too long a journey to come home disappointed. And I thought it would be good for the city. Naively, I had not reckoned on them never letting us forget about it. This was the start of me being "twitter and bisted".

Dukla had a strange history. After being set up by the Czech Army, they first went under the name of A.T.K. In 1953 this was changed to U.D.A. Then in 1956 the club was renamed Dukla in honour of a Slovak village that withstood a German onslaught during World War Two.

The Czech club was only 31 years old. In contrast, it was the Blues' centenary. One hundred years of Everton, now that was something to celebrate, but there was little in the way of pubic events. A reporter on the Liverpool Weekly News asked why the club appeared not to be doing anything to mark this milestone. He was told there had been a shareholders' dinner to commemorate the event.

The second leg took place in Prague in front of a capacity crowd of 28,000 which was four times Dukla's average attendance. Everton obviously knew they had to score but there must have been the nagging thought in the back of their minds that if they let one in, the task would become very difficult.

Dukla had three attackers on the pitch, instead of the two they played at Goodison. The new face was Vizek and he was getting himself into some good positions. He had three efforts on goal before half-time, with one deflected over the bar and two going wide. However Kenyon and, in particular, Wright, were playing well at the heart of the Everton defence.

Billy Wright recalled: "We went out there full of confidence thinking we were going to get a result. But from five or ten minutes into the game, it was backs to the wall."

Dobson was working hard in midfield, matching the Czechs every inch of the way for technical skill. Ross threatened to break the deadlock midway through the second half when he raced down the right flank and put the ball over into the Dukla goalmouth but no Blue shirt was well placed enough to take advantage. The tie was poised on a knife-edge.

Wright said: "We rarely got out of our own half and when we did, we did not create a lot. It was one of those games where it was a question of hanging on, hanging on, battling, trying to get stuff away. It was just wave after wave of attack. Eventually something was going to give. One of their guys scored an absolute cracker."

It was in the 80th minute; the Czechs were awarded a free kick near the Everton goalline. It was taken by Gajdusek whose cross ended up bouncing back to him. He replied with a shot that whistled into the net. Wood recalled: "We were doing well, keeping it at 0-0, Someone headed it out, Roger Kenyon I think, and it went to this fella and he hit it on the volley into the top corner. But by that stage we should have been out of sight. We should have been three or four up from the home leg."

But instead it was now 1-0 on the night to Dukla. and 2-2 on aggregate. If the score stayed that way, Dukla would go through due to their away goal. King, the hero of the derby match, was sitting on the bench with an injury. He was sent on as substitute for Nulty in the hope of conjuring a goal that would put Everton back in the lead, but to no avail. It was the first game Everton had lost since the previous April.

Wood lamented: "We did have a decent side then, always in the top three of the league. We were good going forward, solid at the back. but we always seemed to shoot ourselves in the foot in the cups."

Out of all the clubs that made a name for themselves in European competition, Dukla Prague is probably the one with the shortest lifespan. In late 1989 the country's Communist leaders resigned as demand grew for political reform. The Czech Army remained of course and Dukla were still good enough to win the Cup in 1990. But their major rivals, such as Sparta Prague, began to acquire big sponsorship deals. In contrast, Dukla's funding began to dry up. There was not the same level of commitment from the military and the club's communist heritage was a turn-off for many sponsors. And there were less players to draw on after 1993 when the country split into the Czech Republic and Slovakia. Then the army formally withdrew its support in January 1994. At the end of the season they were relegated. The club's finances were so bad it fell foul of the club licensing system in the Czech Republic and it was dropped to the third division. How the mighty had fallen.

Later a businessman took control of both Third Division Dukla Prague and Second Division FC Pribram, based in a town 60 kilometres southwest of Prague. In 1996 he merged the two into Dukla Pribram and they began playing in the Second Division, using the stadium in Pribram. One Dukla official said the club's departure from Prague was inevitable. "First, the military abandoned us, even though we had been its pride and joy for decades. Then our fans abandoned us. There was no choice."

The club went on to change their name to Marila Pribram, and they got into the top flight of Czech football. But nobody ever sings All I Want for Christmas Is A Marila Pribram Away Kit.

16. NO LEEWAY

Feyenoord
UEFA Cup
1979-80

It was Everton's ninth season in Europe and their sixth in the Fairs Cup or UEFA Cup. Only once had we reached the quarter-finals, in 1970-71. The first hurdle this year was a difficult one, the Dutch club Feyenoord. The first leg would be in their Kuip stadium.

Rotterdam greeted the travelling Evertonians with a surly indifference. The last time a big English club had visited Rotterdam for a European tie, the Dutch had seen the worst fighting there since the Second World War. When Tottenham played Feyenoord in the second leg of the 1974 Uefa Cup final, fighting had ensued which left hundreds injured. The violence was so bad that 30 years later it still registered inclusion on the Feyenoord club's website. It stated that although Feyenoord had won the UEFA Cup, "May the 29th wasn't a joyous day. For the first time the stadium was host to the football hooligans from England. When defeat seemed inevitable, they started fighting and demolishing their section of the stadium, causing many injuries."

There was also rioting by Spurs supporters in the city centre and the locals clearly had not forgotten. Nor had they forgotten that

Feyenoord was the first Dutch club to win the European Cup. Indeed, they were very proud of this feat. Around 25,000 Feyenoord supporters had travelled to Milan to see their team defeat Celtic 2-1 in the 1970 final. What made it all the sweeter was that Ajax had made it to the European Cup final the previous year and had lost. And a few months later Feyenoord won the 1970 World Club Championship, beating Estudiantes over two legs in an encounter which ended in bizarre gamesmanship. The winning goal came from the bespectacled Joop van Daele. In a rage over his goal, an Estudiantes player ripped the Dutchman's glasses off and trampled on them.

The club had been established in 1908 by youngsters who used to play in the Feyenoord neighbourhood of Rotterdam. It was not too long before they won the Dutch championship in 1924. The club grew rapidly, so much so that it was decided to build a stadium with a capacity of 65,000. The Kuip, which opened in 1937, was to later become forever part of Everton.

The Blues had had a dismal start to the season. They had won only two of their first six league games, losing three. They had picked up just one point from their three home games. The game at Goodison the previous Saturday had ended in controversy when Andy King was sent off in a 3-2 defeat by Wolves after pushing Emlyn Hughes who tumbled to the floor where he sat holding his face.

Colin Todd, signed only a year earlier from Derby, had decided to join Birmingham even though it meant dropping down a division. He was unhappy that he did not regularly play at centre back, often being asked to play right back. Asked what he thought of the Everton team, Todd said: "They've got good players but they are always under pressure because of the neighbours next door."

Gordon Lee's recent signings, midfielders Asa Hartford and Gary Stanley, were ineligible. Bob Latchford was injured, having missed the start of the season. Everton took to the field with a rather physical midfield with the tough tackling Trevor Ross, industrious Geoff Nulty and Billy Wright who normally played centre back. The one natural playmaker in the team was Andy King.

At the back, Mick Lyons and Mark Higgins paired up in the middle with John Bailey on their left and John "Dick" Barton on their right. Up front was the lithe Peter Eastoe and Brian Kidd who as a 19-year-old had scored for Manchester United in the 1968 European Cup final. It was a team that was not likely to give much away, but it was not one to be expected to create too much either. The Everton team was: Wood, Barton, Bailey, Lyons, Higgins, Ross, Nulty, Wright, King, Kidd, Eastoe.

The previous weekend Feyenoord had won the Rotterdam derby, beating Sparta, to maintain their unbeaten start to the season. There were around 3,000 Evertonians in the ground, mainly situated near the halfway line, but were heard around the ground. While not a great game, it was an absorbing contest with the two teams being evenly matched. It was one of those games where a superb bit of skill, or a mistake, was liable to be the difference between the two teams.

Feyenoord took the lead midway through the first half when Rene Notten sent in a shot from 20 yards. George Wood appeared to have it covered but the ball seemed to go under his body. "I carried the can for that," said Wood. "I misjudged the shot. It went underneath me."

Of course, he was not the only man on the pitch to make a mistake that night. But errors that result in goals are the ones that are remembered. Everton rallied well, dealing competently with anything else that Feyenoord threw at them and foraging forwards in search of an equaliser. Eastoe and Kidd worked hard up front but the Dutch defence was defiant while goaleeper Ton van Engelen made saves from Wright and Barton. The game finished 1-0.

Wright was impressed with the Feyenoord team: "I remember playing against a very good Dutch side. We were chasing shadows every now and again. They were a very good footballing side, they knocked it about, had movement and everything."

John Moores was now 83 years of age and still the man with the major shareholding in Everton. Some might have thought it was time for the great man to divest himself of the club and pass on control to somebody else. That he did not do so was perhaps because he was having a tricky time arranging an orderly succession of the Littlewoods empire.

After his son Peter had become chairman of Littlewoods, profits had started to fall. They had stood at £49million in 1977, but in 1980 they were to be as low as £11.5million. He felt he had to take the reins back from Peter and so, in 1980, at the age of 84, he was to get actively involved again in the Littlewoods business. Of course, for a man of his years, this could only be a temporary measure.

Before the second leg Feyenoord had a morale-boosting 4-0 win over arch-rivals Ajax. By contrast, Everton had drawn 0-0 at home against Bristol City in front of 24,000, although this had followed a draw at Aston Villa in the League Cup and a 1-1 draw in the league at Ipswich.

Lee was clearly troubled by Everton's lack of goalscoring as he decided to hand a debut to 19-year-old Scottish left-winger Joe McBride who had been on the subs' bench in Rotterdam. His father had played for Jock Stein's Celtic but injury had ruled him out of the European Cup final in Lisbon. Dave Thomas, who had run down the left wing so many times for Everton with his socks rolled down, was on his way out of Goodison. He was choosing between Manchester United and Wolves. "The last couple of months have been terrible but I hope I will leave without any hard feelings," said Thomas who opted for Wolves.

Latchford had now recovered sufficiently to be a substitute but was not considered fit enough to start. Lee's options had been further reduced by a bout of flu which ruled out Ross. The Everton team was: Wood, Barton, Bailey, Lyons, Higgins, Nulty, McBride, Wright, King, Kidd, Eastoe.

Feyenoord coach Vaclav Jezek was familiar with Goodison because six years earlier he had been coach of the Czech national team and had spent time at Bellefield studying the Blues' training methods. "I have been an Everton supporter ever since," he told local reporters.

There was to be a sense of deja vu about Everton's performance that evening. The 28,000 crowd roared the team on, the Blues had the lion's share of possession and created chances but struggled to hit the back of the net. The template was set in the first minute when Bailey and Eastoe linked up well to create an opportunity for Kidd but he shot over the bar.

Everton piled the pressure on although they had to be alert at the back at times as Feyenoord broke with alacrity. Wood kept the Blues in the competition with a fine save in the first half after neat passing between Rene Notten and Wim Jansen.

The Dutch defended well and when Everton created chances they too often snatched at them although Feyenoord had their goalkeeper van Engelen to thank for stopping a Kidd volley. The only goal of the game came when substitute Richard Budding hit a shot from 20 yards that skidded off the damp turf past Wood. It looked uncannily like the goal the Scot had conceded in Rotterdam. Wood recalled: "At Goodison, I got a bit of stick again, but the shot got a bit of a deflection and it just passed my side."

Latchford, on as a substitute, gave the Dutch defence something to think about, but it was another early European exit. In the next round Feyenoord played Borussia Monchengladbach. After drawing 1-1 in the first leg, an estimated 14,000 Feyenoord fans travelled across the border only to see their team lose 3-0.

Looking back, Wood said: "We should have scored in both games. They were a decent side but we should have beaten them over two legs. We dominated at Goodison. We were passing, getting it wide and getting the ball in up front. But then impatience set in, we started getting the ball up too quickly. When that happens, you are always liable to get caught on the break, and that's what happened to us."

A few weeks later Everton went out of the League Cup at Grimsby. Our league form continued to be patchy but we went on a FA Cup run that took us to the semis where we faced West Ham. Brian Kidd put the Blues ahead but minutes later got in a fracas on the touchline with Ray Stewart. The Everton player was sent off, but not his sparring partner. West Ham equalised and won the replay. After that we won only one of our last five league games and finished 19th, one spot above the relegation places.

The Feyenoord defeat was our last, big disappointment of the 1970s. The decade which had started with so much cheer and confidence had been a frustrating one. Even with hindsight, the author is unsure how to view the 1970s. We had been in the running for trophies at regular intervals, so there had been plenty of thrills along the way. Nor did we suffer relegation like some other big clubs in this decade, namely Newcastle, Manchester United, Tottenham and Chelsea, twice. Certainly we did better in the Seventies than the Fifties. But of course the problem was that since we had last won a trophy, the championship in 1970, our loveable neighbours had won the title four times, FA Cup once and the European Cup twice. It was too much to bear. In 1980, I left Merseyside to work away, only to learn that Liverpool now had "supporters" everywhere.

17. RIPPED SAILS

University College Dublin
European Cup Winners Cup
1984-85

FOURTEEN years of hurt came to an end when Everton won their first trophy since 1970. It was the FA Cup and it glistened and twinkled as 23-year-old captain Kevin Ratcliffe held it aloft in the royal box at Wembley after the 2-0 defeat of Watford.

The triumph in May 1984 came at the end of Howard Kendall's third season as manager. It was as if he was a scientist, tinkering and testing as he tried to find the magic formula to re-create Goodison glory. It was as if someone had thrown away the formula in 1970 and a new one was needed to work in a different era. Kendall was not a mad scientist, but he had become a mad Evertonian, and he suffered a number of disappointments in his quest. At times there were calls to replace him with a new alchemist, but he persevered, with the aid of his assistant Mick Heaton. It was in the first few months of 1984 that he must have been tempted to shout "Eureka!" The team began to play in a more flowing manner and with much greater assurance. When the season ended with Ratcliffe turning in the royal box to salute the Everton fans, the FA Cup did not just glisten and twinkle, it also winked.

I don't think Graeme Sharp realised how good it was to see his goal against Watford. Remarkably, in our last three appearances in Wembley finals - 1984 League Cup, 1977 League Cup and 1968 FA Cup - we had failed to score, so it was the first Everton goal at Wembley in 18 years.

As the draw for the first round of the Cup Winners Cup approached, an old joke had been resurrected by the Kopites. "Everton have been banned from Europe because the last time they went they ripped the sails and threw the cannons overboard."

Yet we could have travelled in an old sailing ship to our first opponents, just 100 miles away in Dublin. The name of our opponents produced smiles on Everton faces. English clubs who have drawn Irish teams in Europe have always looked upon their opponents as minnows. But even Irish clubs looked upon University College Dublin as minnows.

UCD had just caused a huge upset in Irish football by winning the cup, beating Shamrock Rovers, Dublin's top club, who had won the League of Ireland that year. When the "students" held Rovers to a draw in the final at Tolka Park, it was felt that the chance of an upset had gone. Rovers would not slip up again. But in the replay, the underdogs triumphed 2-1 with goals from Joe Hanrahan and Ken O'Doherty. As if to underline what a shock result it was, Shamrock went on to do the Irish double in the next three seasons.

So when Everton travelled to Dublin, the supporters believed that it was merely a question of how many goals the Blues would score. Expecting a big turn-out, especially with several thousand Evertonians coming, UCD switched the game from their own modest ground to Tolka Park. In the stands were Tommy Eglington and Peter Farrell who had played for Everton and not one Ireland, but two Irelands.

The two had played together for Shamrock Rovers until 1946 when they were bought by Everton for a fee reported to be £10,000. The Blues got more than their money's worth. Farrell played 422 league matches for Everton and was team captain for seven seasons. Eglington, an outside left, made 428 appearances for Everton in 11 years, rattling in 82 goals, including five in one game against Doncaster in 1952.

The 1950s was the first decade that Irish football supporters began regularly travelling over to England in large numbers just to see a football match. Very few could afford to fly but they could get the money together for the overnight boats that sailed from Dublin and Belfast to Liverpool. Everton were known for their Irish players in the Fifties. There was not only Farrell and Eglington, but also goalkeeper Jimmy O'Neill, full back Tommy Clinton and versatile players such as Dan Donovan and Mick Meagan. This fine collection made Everton probably the best supported English club in Ireland. There was even more Irish interest in Everton when Johnny Carey became manager in 1958. This of course was the time when Liverpool were a Second Division team. Eglington recalled the popularity of his club side at the time: "Back in the 50s, Everton was the team in Ireland. We had a number of Irish players then and the boats would be full of fans coming over every Friday night."

Among them was young Bobby Eager, from Dublin, "It would take about 11 hours on the boat. It would leave Dublin at 8pm and get into Liverpool at 7am. But first it would stop off at Birkenhead and let the cattle off.

"The boat would be packed out, sometimes with supporters of different teams, and the banter used to be terrific. There would be a lot of gargle (drinking) and playing of cards. Occasionally the old beer and cards used to start a few rows. But there was security on the boat and if there was any trouble they used to lock them up with the cows; there was a little room beside them.

"I would go with my father who always insisted on getting a cabin. After getting off the boat in Liverpool, we would walk up to the Punch and Judy cafe and have a bit of breakfast. Then we would have a walk around the city centre, or go over on the ferry to Birkenhead market. Then we would be up to the game in plenty of time for kick-off.

"Now and again we would go to Manchester or Sheffield to watch a game - my dad just used to like watching a game and he considered himself a Leeds fan - so on those days after getting off the boat in Liverpool, we would get a train. After the game, we would get the boat back on Saturday night. We'd be knackerred when we got home on Sunday," said Eager who now flies over for games.

The considerable number of Dublin accents at Goodison in the Fifties - on the pitch, in the dugout and on the terraces - probably contributed to the theory that Everton were the Catholic club in the city, which is a strange one given that the origins of the club were in a Methodist church, St Domingo's. When this theory started is not clear. It may have been due to the fact that some areas such as Bootle and Old Swan, which traditionally had large Catholic populations, were also known to have many Everton supporters. Even today, football supporters from outside Merseyside occasionally ask if Everton are the Protestant or Catholic club in Liverpool. The answer is that today religion has very, very little influence, if any at all, in determining what team a Merseysider supports. What's more, Blues already do enough arguing with Reds, without throwing in needless religious connotations.

But in the early 1970s, there was a phase where some Liverpool supporters demonstrated an affinity to Glasgow Rangers. It was mainly among teenagers and quite a few Kopites could be seen going to the match, wearing not just their red scarves, but Rangers scarves too, which looked a bit strange because they were predominantly blue. One of these scarves would be worn around the neck while the other might be tied round the wrist, or waistband. Soon a similar number of Blues could be seen with green and white Celtic scarves. As with so many fashions, it faded away, especially after Liverpool signed Kenny Dalglish from Celtic in 1977. Thus began a gradual rapprochement which has led to the situation today where Celtic and Liverpool fans sing each other's songs. So if you know your history, it's enough to make you confused.

And it was confusing that night in Tolka Park in September 1984. The FA Cup winners could not beat the Irish part-timers. UCD defended superbly, with an inspirational display by centre half Paddy Dunning. Derek Mountfield, who played at the heart of the Everton defence in 1984, recalled: "It was meant to be the easiest of starts. I remember going into the game feeling full of confidence. Over there we should have won but we just could not score."

But Kevin Ratcliffe was not totally surprised. In his 1988 autobiography The Blues and I, Ratcliffe described UCD as a team, "we would probably beat 999 times out of a thousand".

"But this wasn't a matter of form or quality," he added. "It wouldn't have mattered who we faced in that first round. It was the first European club game for all of us and we dreaded making a mess of it. Everton's record in Europe had not been good."

Two years older than Mountfield, another boyhood Evertonian, Ratcliffe remembered only too well that in 1970-71 the Blues had beaten a great German team then failed to dispose of an unfancied Greek team that scraped past them on the away goals rule.

By the time the second leg came around, Evertonians had realised that UCD were not just a bunch of students, who had just got out of bed. It was UCD's sixth season in the League of Ireland and they had decided some time ago that in order to survive in the top flight in the Republic of Ireland, places in the team could not be confined to students. By 1984 most of its players had been recruited from other League of Ireland clubs. Dunning, for example, had played for Shelbourne and Dundalk.

But still hopes were high of a Goodison goal-fest against UCD. Everton had warmed up the previous Saturday by scoring five away in a nine-goal thriller at Graham Taylor's Watford.

Little more than 10 minutes had elapsed at Goodison when, following neat play by Trevor Steven and Adrian Heath, Graeme Sharp breached the Irish defence to put Everton in the lead. Evertonians braced themselves for an avalanche of goals. But although there was almost 80 minutes of play left, there was not to be another goal until eight days later when we played Sheffield United in the League Cup.

Ratcliffe wrote: "If we were edgy over there, it was worse at Goodison. I was really uptight and Reidy even worse. We were terrified of being caught on the break and conceding an away goal."

The Dubliners defended and defended and defended. Everton huffed and puffed as UCD got every man they could behind the ball. Of course, the Blues did manage to create chances but goalkeeper Alan O'Neill, a civil servant, showed why he had been voted man of the match in both of UCD's cup final games against Shamrock. He pulled off fine save after fine save with monotonous regularity. It was not only frustrating, but bewildering for the 16,000 crowd. The Everton players left the field to a chorus of boos and jeers from their supporters who felt they had let down the name of Hafnia, the cooked meats firm whose named was emblazoned on the Everton shirts.

Mountfield recalled: "UCD came back over here knowing that one away goal for them could be all-important. And I remember Nev made a smart save late on to keep it at 1-0, otherwise it would have been 1-1. It was probably the hardest two games we played all the way through the tournament."

18. BLUE DANUBE WALTZ

Inter Bratislava
European Cup Winners Cup
1984-85

The next round took Everton to Eastern Europe. The opponents were Inter Bratislava who were very much an unknown quantity. It was only six years earlier that Everton had visited Czechoslovakia to play Dukla Prague. But the Czech Army team had a reputation that went before them. So little was known about Inter Bratislava that some Evertonians initially confused them with the better known Slovan Bratislava who had made many forays into Europe over the years. The first leg was to be played in Bratislava, which stands on the River Danube, the inspiration for Johann Strauss's Blue Danube Waltz.

Before travelling to Bratislava, the Blues enjoyed a 3-0 win over Leicester which put them on top of the league for the first time in more than five years. Evertonians were thrilled with the way the team was playing. Everton were putting together glorious performances in the league, week after week. It seemed too good to be true. But the delight was entwined with deep frustration for 29-year-old Alan Wynne, who had followed the Blues around the country through the Seventies and early Eighties. Just as the beautiful dawn rose of the mid-Eighties' Everton team, so Alan entered a world of darkness. He was a diabetic and his sight had begun to fail. The glory days had returned, but he could not see them.

Alan, who had grown up on the Mill Park estate, in Eastham, Wirral, said in 1998: "My dad wasn't interested in football but my grandad was a fanatical Evertonian and he took me to my first game, against Tranmere in the FA Cup in 1968. My mum and dad wouldn't let me go to a game on my own and in those days your parents got their way. But there was a lad in class called Chrissie Bird who supported Manchester United and he had been to more Man United games than I had to Everton matches. Everyone in class was taking the mickey out of me so I thought 'I love Everton, I am not going to miss another game.'"

"And so I missed only one home game between 1968 and 1983. That was against Leicester, who had Peter Shilton in goal, and we won 7-1. I knew which match to miss. I also went to plenty of away matches, whenever I had the money. I loved it. After 1970, though, Everton were a disaster.

"The trouble was we had reached such great heights in the Sixties and especially 1970 when we won the league. It was a team of riches. I still dream about them. I can still see Ball, Kendall and Harvey flicking the ball, contemptuously, between players' legs."

"After that, we still had a lot of great players, like Andy King, Duncan McKenzie and Martin Dobson who would give you moments of brilliance. And we had great artisans like Mick Lyons and Terry Darracott, local people who would were prepared to give their life for the team. And through the Seventies we challenged for the league and got to semi-finals and finals. But of course it all fell away as it always did with Everton.

"Then in 1983 my sight started to fail. I still used to go to games for a while, like the FA Cup final in 1984 and some league games in 1984-85 when we won the title. But I could not enjoy it. If you are there and can't see it, it is the most empty feeling. It was like having my garden full of beautiful flowers and beautiful birds and being inches away from them but not being able to see them."

Inter Bratislava had been beaten finalists in the Czechoslovakian Cup. This competition did not begin until 1960, presumably so that Czechoslovakia could enter a team in the newly created Cup Winners Cup. The Czechoslovakian Cup final was always between the Czech Cup winners and the Slovakian Cup holders. In 1984 Inter had won the Slovakian Cup, beating Dukla Banska Bystrica over two legs, but then lost to Sparta Prague who had also won the Czechoslovakian League and chosen to enter the European Cup.

Inter Bratislava had only been formed in 1950. It began as a sports club which did not play football at first. But within a few years it was playing in Czechoslovakia's top division. The vital factor was the financial backing of the state-run oil company Slovnaft which has a huge refinery in Bratislava. "Slovnaft was the main reason for the establishment of this club," said an Inter spokesman in 2000. "It was from Slovnaft that the whole club really grew and got to the position we are in today. We call it our mother."

The Blues did not dare take Inter lightly. Although there was television coverage of European football in the mid-80s, there were then far fewer TV channels and they gave far less time to the game. As a result, players tended to know very little about their opponents.

Derek Mountfield said: "It was always hard with the opening game. There would be a little bit of apprehension. The managers and coaches would have the opposing teams watched and have some idea of what to expect. They would try and pass that on, but for players there was still a feeling of going out on the pitch to meet an unknown quantity. So a lot of those games in those days were cat and mouse, working out what they were like. But these days, with the huge amount of television coverage of European football, players know about virtually every other player in the opposing team."

Pat Van den Hauwe was ineligible for the second round and John Bailey was recalled to the left back spot by Howard Kendall who had been named manager of the month for October 1984. There was a crowd of around 15,000 in Bratislava. The Everton team was: Southall, Stevens, Bailey, Ratcliffe, Mountfield, Reid, Steven, Heath, Sharp, Bracewell, Harper.

The Blues got just the start they wanted with a collector's item of a goal, a header from Paul Bracewell, in the sixth minute. If nerves needed settling, that goal did the trick. It allowed the Blues to sit back a little more and be more patient in seeing what the Slovaks had to offer.

As the game wore on, the travelling Evertonians realised that Inter were not in the same class as the Dukla Prague team that had at times ran the Blues ragged. Twice in the first half the Slovaks did get into dangerous positions but they shot wide. Bracewell, Peter Reid, and Alan Harper were snuffing out some Inter attacks before they had barely started. Trevor Steven meanwhile was floating down the right flank to pose problems for the Slovaks' backline who were looking increasingly Straussed out.

The second half followed a similar pattern. Everton felt no great need to push forward in numbers, although they would have gratefully accepted a second goal. There were several attempts on the Everton goal and Neville Southall had to be alert to deal with a long-range shot from Mraz, but Kendall's team always looked in control. Forgive the puns, but the game on the Danube was a waltz for the Blues.

"We gave them credit for being a better team than they were and played accordingly," said Kevin Ratcliffe in his book, The Blues and I. The Welshman added that what stretched the Everton players the most in Bratislava was the walk along the longest players' tunnel he had ever known.

Mountfield said: "We were pretty comfortable over there. You always looked to go away and come back with a clean slate. So, having got a 1-0 win, we came back quite happy."

Meanwhile Sir John Moores, knighted in 1980, had finally retired from Littlewoods. This followed his appointment of an outsider to run the Littlewoods empire. Chief executive Desmond Pitcher had made a name for himself as a no-nonsense boss, first at Leyland Vehicles then Plessey.

Moores was no longer a director at Goodison. He was happy to leave the overseeing of Everton to Philip Carter, who was midway through a 13-year spell as club chairman, and to club secretary Jim Greenwood.

Under Carter's chairmanship, the board had appointed Kendall as manager and resisted calls for the young manager's dismissal when he was still struggling to find the right formula. Having retired from Littlewoods in 1983, at the age of 56, Carter had more time to devote to Everton. He also became an increasingly influential figure in public life, becoming chairman of Merseyside Conservative Association in 1985, chairman of Merseyside Tourism Board and of Empire Theatre Trust in 1986, and chairman of the Government's Merseyside Development Corporation in 1987. All these positions he held for several years.

As chairman of Everton, there were many challenges to confront, most notably the issue of televised football which had become a battleground in the mid-80s. It later emerged that the "Big Five" - Everton, Arsenal, Tottenham, Manchester United and Liverpool - had been holding talks about the possibility of breaking away to form their own "super league" which would strike its own television deal, reaping millions of pounds.

Everton were represented in these talks by Carter, who often appeared to be the spokesman of the group. It is inconceivable that he would have ventured into these talks without the approval of Sir John. And Carter's prominent role suggests that the initiative may even have originated from Goodison. Was Moores - the man of vision with an eye for future trends - the architect of this proposed breakaway which eventually led to the formation of the Premiership?

The Blues were going exceedingly well in the autumn of 1984 but it was a frustrating time for club captain Mark Higgins. The centre half was meeting a specialist over the groin injury that had kept him out of action for most of 1984 and had ruled him out of our two Wembley cup finals that year. The League Cup final was notable for the subtle goalkeeping skills of Liverpool's Alan Hansen whose goalline handball was not spotted by the referee, even though we could clearly see it from the other end of Wembley. The game finished goalless and we lost the replay.

On the day before the second leg against Bratislava, the Slovaks' pre-match preparations were disrupted when their flight was delayed by three hours. They had hoped to pay a visit to Goodison and have a training session but these plans had to be scrapped. On the day of the game, some of their players chose to unwind by going shopping in the city centre. It was the only way they were going to return home with anything. The Everton team was:

Southall, Stevens, Mountfield, Ratcliffe, Bailey, Steven, Reid, Bracewell, Sheedy, Heath, Sharp.

There was a crowd of around 25,000 at Goodison. Younger supporters may be surprised that the average attendance in what was a championship season was little more than 32,000 even though the capacity was 51,000. And that was a big improvement on 1983-84 when the average was 19,288. The long wait for a trophy had sapped the Goodison morale. But football was not fashionable at this point in time, due partly to the frequent clashes between rival supporters which led to fences being erected at grounds.

The second leg started in the same manner as the first with Everton scoring an early goal; again it was a header, this time from Graeme Sharp. Still, if Bratislava could win the game 2-1, they would go through on the away goals rule. The first half ebbed and flowed but Everton looked the more threatening and created far more chances; they also spurned a lot more opportunities than Bratislava. Memories of missed chances at Goodison against Dukla Prague might have ran through some minds. But the pressure was taken off Kendall's half-time talk when Kevin Sheedy - whose left foot was really a magic wand - scored a minute before the interval. It was 2-0 on the night and 3-0 on aggregate. The Slovaks would have to score three without reply in the second half. If there was any doubt about the outcome, it was dispelled by a goal on 63 minutes from Adrian Heath.

The game turned into a canter. Kendall decided to rest Reid and replace him with Harper for the last 20 minutes. In the 78th minute, Kendall sent on a youngster whose father had played in 17 European ties for Everton. Johnny Morrissey junior did not have too long to show what he could do, but it meant he had played a part in Everton's Cup Winners Cup run.

19. STREAKER LUCK

Fortuna Sittard
European Cup Winners Cup
1984-85

The draw for the quarter-finals was fortuitous for Everton. Instead of being pitted against Roma or Bayern Munich, the Blues got Fortuna Sittard. Roma might have been problematic outside the stadium as well as on the pitch. The previous year Liverpool had travelled there to play in the European Cup final. Such was UEFA's ability to arrange a neutral venue that the opponents were Roma. After Liverpool's win, their supporters were confronted by gangs of local hooligans who launched a series of violent attacks.

Our Dutch opponents had no famous players except for one who had played against the Blues on several occasions. Franz Thijssen was one of the first foreign players to make a major impact in the English league. During his spell with Ipswich under Bobby Robson, the Dutchman was even named Footballer of the Year in 1981. Fortuna had qualified for the tournament as beaten cup finalists, having lost 1-0 to Feyenoord who had also won the league. Fortuna had not started the new season too well, but had picked up and managed to put some good results together. Their coach Bert

Jacobs had taken his squad to Benidorm for a training session in February and, publicly at least, he was confident about meeting Everton. "I believe we can cause a surprise and get through," he said.

Thijssen was one of only a handful of full-time players on the club's books. Most were semi-professionals who had jobs to hold down, or college courses to follow. Training sessions were held in the evening. However they had performed well to get this far. In the first round Fortuna had knocked out the Danish club BK Kopenhagen, drawing away 0-0 then winning the return 3-0. In the second round they defeated Wisla Krakow at home 2-0 then travelled to Poland where they scraped through, losing 2-1 on the night but winning 3-2 on aggregate. So they were no mugs, as they proved in the first half at Goodison. The Everton team was: Southall, Stevens, Van den Hauwe, Ratcliffe, Mountfield, Reid, Steven, Curran, Gray, Bracewell, Sheedy.

The Fortuna defence was well organised and their big centre-half Wim Koevermans was winning on points in his personal battle with Andy Gray. Most of the Sittard players were relatively inexperienced and it was a treat for them to play at a big ground such as Goodison Park. But they rose to the occasion, frustrating Everton who looked below par as they struggled to make any real inroads. Arthur Hoyer posed an occasional threat to the Blues defence but Fortuna rarely looked like scoring. The crowd of 26,000 was rather disappointed.

But just a few minutes into the second half, Gray broke the deadlock, pouncing to stab the ball home after goalkeeper Van Gervan failed to hold a shot from Peter Reid who later limped off with a groin strain to be replaced by Kevin Richardson. Still the Dutch kept plugging away, making life difficult for Everton. They were less than 20 minutes away from taking Everton back to Sittard with only a one-goal deficit to overcome.

But, as in the second half of so many games at Goodison, Everton launched wave after wave of attack on the Gwladys Street goal. And from a low cross from Terry Curran, Gray dived to head home from knee-height. Such was the look of astonishment on the goalkeeper's face, it seemed for one moment he would need treatment for shock.

A third goal came a few minutes later. Paul Bracewell put in a solid tackle in the centre circle. He passed to Kevin Sheedy who sent in a swirling cross that Gray met with superb timing to lash into the net. The game finished 3-0. Thijssen said: "We didn't get many chances but we didn't give many away. Everton didn't look very good in the first half so we thought at half-time we were in with a chance."

A few days later, Everton played Ipswich at Goodison in a FA Cup tie. Among the spectators was Harry Catterick who collapsed with a heart attack and died, aged 65. He had also suffered a heart attack during his managerial days, in 1972. Quite possibly, the pressure of being Blues' boss for more than a decade had taken its toll on the great man.

Everton travelled to Sittard as English league leaders, ahead of Tottenham, and we would go on to win the title. Similar to 1970, it was a very English team. But perhaps the most interesting facet was how cheaply Kendall had put together a championship side.

English football fans had seen the first £1million transfer fee in 1979 when Nottingham Forest bought Trevor Francis from Birmingham. But only once in the six years since then had Everton paid out more than half a million for a player. In 1983 Everton paid Stoke £700,000 for Adrian Heath.

Kendall's second most expensive purchase in the championship team was Trevor Steven at £300,000, followed by Gray and Bracewell at £250,000. The others had been brought for sums ranging from £150,000 for Neville Southall to £30,000 for Derek Mountfield, or had come through the club's youth ranks, which was the case with Richardson, Gary Stevens and Kevin Ratcliffe, or they had been liberated from Anfield, as was the case with Sheedy and Alan Harper.

The latter was very under-rated, but very effective in a variety of positions. As for Sheedy, his name would be chanted as soon as Everton got a free kick within sight of the opponents' goal. He did not kick the ball with his left foot, he caressed it, and the ball looked lovely in the back of the net. As for his right foot, that was only there to make up the numbers.

Regards the cost of the 1984-85 team it should be added that Kendall inherited left-back John Bailey, a £300,000 purchase by Gordon Lee, who made 15 league appearances in the championship campaign, and that Kendall was able to go out that season and buy Paul Wilkinson and Ian Atkins to strengthen the squad. That he had the money to buy these players - and Pat Van den Hauwe, bought in September 1984 for £100,000 - was probably due in part to the financial boost from having reached two Wembley finals in 1984.

Not that all of Kendall's purchases worked out wonderfully well. On his arrival in May 1981, he quickly spent around £1million on five players - Alan Biley, Mick Ferguson, Alan Ainscow, Mickey Thomas and Mike Walsh - but none of them stayed more than two seasons.

In March 1985 however Blues supporters were absolutely delighted at the progress of the team. But there was surprise and some annoyance when it was announced that Everton would not be selling any tickets for the away leg. In effect, Everton were banning their own supporters. Even the Fortuna manager Bert Jacobs seemed surprised, pointing out that his club was expecting Everton support from the British Army bases not far from the town, just a short journey across the German border.

Of course, club officials did not think the ban would stop all Evertonians from travelling to Sittard. They knew some would still go. Among them was Donny MacKechnie who looks back on Sittard as his favourite Everton away trip. "We were really, really made welcome. There was a great atmosphere because the game coincided with a special market day which was a once a year celebration. We never had any trouble. They were all wondering why we were banned."

He added: "We went by train and got there early in the morning. We got our tickets for the match at Fortuna's ground; it wasn't a problem whatsoever. We had about a quarter of an away end, in the corner. There was a lot of servicemen there too, who had come from Germany. Most were just Brits who had come to see a game of football. After the game, the vast majority of Blues slept on the train station then we went home the next day."

Fortuna Sittard had a history like a family tree. It had been formed in 1968 in a merger of Fortuna '54 from the town of Geleen and Sittardia from the town of Sittard. But even before this, Sittardia had been born out of two clubs. They dated back to the formation in 1902 of Sittardia Boys who in 1950 had merged with VV Sittard to form Sittardia Sittard.

In the first two years after the 1968 merger, Fortuna Sittard had two homes and took it in turns to play at either De Baandert in Sittard or the Maurits Stadium in Geleen. But they settled in

1970 in Sittard whose business leaders reportedly showed more interest in backing the club. In 1999, Fortuna Sittard moved into another new home, the Wagner & Partners Stadion in Sittard, with a capacity of 12,500.

There was a noisy crowd of 20,000 in the De Baandert stadium for the visit of Everton. Hat-trick hero Gray was out, replaced by Sharp who had missed the first leg through injury. The Everton team was: Southall, Stevens, Van den Hauwe, Ratcliffe, Mountfield, Reid, Steven, Curran, Sharp, Harper, Richardson.

Harper, replacing Bracewell, was in central midfield alongside Reid. The pair were terrier-like, relentless in their approach, stylish in their execution. Steven was on the right flank and as usual he glided across the pitch like an angel floating over clouds. Mountfield recalled: "In the second leg it was a case of not doing anything stupid; not looking straight away for an away goal. We had to be professional and we put in a good, solid performance."

But it was not long before Everton got an away goal. Only a quarter of an hour had passed when Reid tackled Chris Dekkar, won the ball and pushed it to Sharp who beat stand-in keeper Chris Korver. Fortuna did not collapse but pulled out a more physical approach that tested Everton's physical resolve. They were well up to the test.

The Dutch thought for a moment that they had scored when Arthur Hoyer powered a header towards goal but the ball thudded off the bar. At half-time the score was 4-0 on aggregate to the Blues who were looking very composed. The Dutch needed to score five times in the second half against an Everton defence that had not conceded a goal in the tournament that season. The biggest lapse to the Blues' defence came when a Dutch fan decided to run across the pitch naked. "When the streaker came on, police let the dog go," said Mountfield. "I've never seen a streaker run as fast as he did." The dog did not manage to get his teeth into anything, the streaker luckily clambering up the fence just in time.

If there was any lingering, wild optimism among the Dutch fans about a sensational comeback, it was killed off by Reid 15 minutes from time when he got into the box and scored from an acute angle. It was 2-0 to Everton on the night and 5-0 on aggregate. Kendall decided to rest Sharp and put on a promising young centre-forward from the reserves. Rob Wakenshaw who had scored a gem of a goal against Manchester United the previous season. He had a 15-minute run-out. It was the Blues' second substitution. Atkins had replaced Ratcliffe after an hour.

After the game club secretary Jim Greenwoood said: "The big worry was never about our supporters, but the reaction of the Dutch fans in such an accessible country. We still feel we were right to make that decision on tickets, but it's important to add that the people who came across were perfectly behaved and a credit to the club." And they kept their clothes on too.

20. THE NOISE

Bayern Munich
European Cup Winners Cup
1984-85

Bayern Munich were Germany's top club in the Eighties, winning the Bundesliga six times in ten years, including 1985. Consequently the semi-final was a mouth-watering prospect because Everton were looking invincible, outclassing opponents week after week. Sometimes it would take the Blues a while to break down a resolute defence, but rarely did they fail. What made it all the more pleasing was that Everton were playing absolutely superb football. It wasn't quite as good as earlier in the season when Adrian Heath and Graeme Sharp were linking up like a pair of telepathic Brazilians. With Andy Gray in the team, replacing the injured "Inchy", the style up front was a little more direct. However if Gray lacked the subtle skills of Heath, he brought a gusto to the team that spurred on his teammates and whipped up the fans.

The national press had been slow to lavish praise on the resurgent Blues. But most of the pundits were waking up to the fact that a fantastic team had been assembled although one or two ridiculously referred to the Blues as "workmanlike". They may have had in mind the engine room where stokers Peter Reid and

Paul Bracewell were blue-hot every game. Reid was to receive the recognition he deserved, playing for the Everton-England XI in the 1986 World Cup finals, but Bracewell remained an unsung hero, under-rated even by some Evertonians. He was the Oliver Twist of the team, stealing the ball for the benefit of others but never getting his just deserts. Most of the passes he played were short ones, but intelligent ones that ignited another Everton attack. However the 50-yard crossfield ball he played for Trevor Steven in the 4-1 win over Sunderland on the Saturday before the trip to Munich showed just what a marvellous player he was. If Hollywood had made a film of the '85 Everton team they would have shown this glorious pass in slow motion, interspersed with shots of stunned spectators' faces, with music from Tchaikovsky – it was that good.

Surprisingly, given that Bayern had won the European Cup in three successive seasons in the Seventies, they had not been among the founding members of the Bundesliga in 1963. The league's founders had decided that its member clubs would be licensed and all regions of West Germany would be represented. As soon as one club from a region was licensed to join, the number of neighbouring clubs allowed in was restricted. In front of Bayern were arch-rivals TSV Munich 1860 who had won the regional Oberliga in 1963.

TSV, the Blues of Munich, then had their greatest flush of success, winning the German Cup in 1964, reaching the final of the European Cup Winners Cup in 1965, then in 1966 winning the Bundesliga for the only time, before going downhill rapidly.

Bayern, the Reds of Munich, were elevated to the Bundesliga in 1965 with Tasmania Berlin. While the former went from strength to strength, the latter were lifted in for political reasons and bombed spectacularly. Hertha had been the West Berlin club that had joined the Bundesliga as a founder member. But West Berlin was a NATO-protected enclave inside Soviet-controlled East Germany and Hertha were struggling to recruit and retain top quality players. Subsequently Bundesliga officials found irregularities relating to the paying of Hertha players and the club was demoted. In order to maintain a Berlin presence in the Bundesliga, Tasmania were promoted, even though there were doubts over whether they were up to it. They won only two out of 34 games, scoring 15 goals and letting in 108.

In contrast, Bayern had within two years of entering the Bundesliga won a European trophy. Franz Beckenbauer was a member of the Bayern team that won the Cup Winners Cup in 1967. Two years later Bayern did the domestic double, winning the Bundesliga and German Cup. Top scorer was the young Gerd Muller. The Seventies were to be even greater for Bayern. They won the Bundesliga in 1972, 1973 and 1974. As if that was not good enough, they won the European Cup in 1974, 1975 and 1976. To cap it all, they won the World Club Championship in 1976. Beckenbauer and Muller were central figures in this Bayern golden era and figured prominently too when West Germany won the World Cup in 1974. So it is still galling for TSV fans to be reminded that the boy Beckenbauer had been a keen 1860 fan. The promising youngster was all set to join his boyhood club but, the story goes, he had an altercation in a schoolboy team game with a TSV player who clipped him round the ear. In a fit of pique he instead joined Bayern who at that time were no better than 1860. Of course he was not the last boyhood Blue to go and play for the reds. Keen Evertonians Ian Rush, Robbie Fowler, Steve MacManaman, Michael Owen and Jamie Carragher did the same. The only explanation I can offer is that they were all abducted by aliens and given brain implants, instructing them to join Liverpool.

Bayern struck lucky too with Muller, a boyhood Nuremburg fan, who in 427 Bundesliga appearances scored 365 goals for Bayern.

He was the Bundesliga's leading scorer in seven seasons between 1967 and 1978. He joined Bayern as an 18-year-old in 1964, having begun his career in his home town of Nördlingen, and spent 15 years with Bayern.

Another of the Bayern greats in the Seventies was the mazy dribbler Uli Hoeness but he was forced to retire in 1979 at the age of 27. Such was the respect for Hoeness that he was offered a place in the management team and in 1985 he was the club's general manager. He was to move on to become deputy chairman. Notably, Beckenbauer too became a hugely powerful figure in the Bayern boardroom. Would Everton have benefited from promoting, say, Brian Labone or Howard Kendall to the board of directors?

When Everton were drawn against Bayern, John Shearon, from Norris Green, Liverpool, was 25 years old and working in Bilbao, teaching English to 19-year-old Basque girls on secretarial courses. He needed a break. He took a train to Paris, slept on the station in the French capital for a few hours, caught a train to Stuttgart then a connecting service to Munich, arriving on the morning of the game.

The journey was a piece of cake for Shearon. A few years earlier he had been studying Spanish in Mexico City and hitchhiked through South America so he could visit the home of the Chilean club called Everton.

In the railway station in Munich he was able to buy a ticket for the game, in the Everton section, before checking into a hotel. He said: "I remember meeting up with some Everton fans I knew and we went to the famous beer hall, the Hofbrahaus, but they wouldn't let us in unless we took our Everton scarves off, which we did. Then we walked in and everyone was wearing Everton scarves."

He added: "At the game there was about 100 or so lads all in blue and white at the very top of the away section, all talking German. I went up to speak to them. They were all 1860 Munich fans. They were a bit like us, living in the shadow of a team dominant in Europe but still keeping going."

But it had been far worse for them. TSV's Bundesliga title of 1965 remains their only one, and four years later they had been relegated. On this evening in 1985 they were in the third tier of German football. In 1981 they had finished 16th in the Bundesliga and were relegated. In the following season, due to financial problems and the strict club licensing system in Germany, TSV were dropped a further tier into the Bayernliga. They spent nine seasons in the third tier. It was not until 1991 that they got back into the second tier, Bundesliga Sud (South) and not until 1994 that they got back in the top flight. In 2000 they finished fourth and qualified for the UEFA Cup, but in 2004 they were relegated again.

There was a crowd of 70,000 in the Olympic Stadium, which had been built for the 1974 Games. Gray was injured and so Steven was partnering Sharp up front. In the first quarter Everton had to withstand intense Bayern pressure. Michael Rummenigge almost scored but Kevin Richardson kicked the ball off the line. Everton were able to come out of their shell in the second half and Sharp had a chance to nick the game.

Derek Mountfield recalled: "We had to dig deep and we did just that. People may say we rode our luck a little bit, I remember Richo cleared one off the line, but we performed exceptionally well. At the end the Everton fans were dancing up and down like lunatics. They were on Cloud Nine. I remember talking to some later that night who reckoned we were through, but we were not convinced. We thought we had to be careful in the second leg."

In between were two league games, a 4-1 win over West Brom at Goodison and a 2-0 win at Stoke where Evertonians were crammed into pens, and yet more and more were herded in; the author can still recall the discomfort and not a little anxiety at the increasing crush.

The visit of Bayern Munich in April 1985 is generally considered to be one of the best ever games at Goodison Park. There was suspense, drama, goals and, most of all, noise – decibels of delirium. I can remember deciding to mentally switch off from the game in the second half, diverting my gaze for ten seconds or so, just to concentrate on absorbing the noise. It is not chanting or singing that sticks in my mind, it is the sound of what seemed like 40,000 Evertonians just shouting, at each other, at the players, which resulted in a synphonia of delirium.

Mountfield recalled: "Ask all the Everton players in that team what was their most memorable game and nine out of ten will say the Bayern game. I remember before the game, around about 6.15pm, the team bus went down the back of the Street End and we could not move. There was just so many people there." Quite simply, it was one of the great European nights at Goodison.

"It was a pretty open game in the first half," said Mountfield. In midfield, Reid and the Dane Soren Lerby were having a fierce battle. One tackle cut Reid's leg badly. The Blues' physiotherapist John Clinkard told him he needed stitches. Ratcliffe wrote in his 1988 autobiography: "Reidy knew the German bench were watching closely and didn't want to show any sign of weakness. He picked up a sponge, jammed it inside his bloodied sock, saying 'This'll do', and went back to the battle as if nothing had happened."

The Germans were strong and solid. In the 38th minute they took the lead through Dieter Hoeness following good work by the winger Ludwig Kogl. Mountfield recalled: "They scored from our corner; they just broke away."

It was a classic away goal. Obviously the thought that ran through the minds of many Evertonians was: "Is this going to be another case of European heartbreak?"

In the second half Everton would be kicking towards the Gwladys Street end, the most vocal section of the crowd. Goodison had been noisy in the first half but Kendall knew he could rely on the Street End to crank the volume up further. Everton had given many exhibitions through the season of artistic football, but not tonight. Kendall wanted his team to get the ball into the Bayern box as much as possible and as quickly as possible.

Within three minutes the policy had paid off with a goal from Sharp. The noise, not just from the Gwladys Street, but the whole ground, was awesome, keeping children awake not just in Walton, but Walsall and Warsaw. Following his goals in the previous two rounds, the 24-year-old Scot became only the third Everton player - after Fred Pickering and Johnny Morrissey - to score against three different clubs in Europe.

The score was now 1-1, on the night and on aggregate. With two Glaswegian centre forwards, our attack was bound to be uncompromising. The physical combat that Gray and Sharp were having with Hans Pfugler and Norbert Eder had led to the spilling of blood on shirts. It has gone into Everton legend that at one point, Bayern general manager Uli Hoeness turned to the Everton bench and said: "This is not football, Mr Kendall." Apparently, the reply was brief.

The crowd was in a frenzy, so much so that some of the chants were starting in the normally reserved airs of the Main Stand. The old guys in the Bullens Road stands had ripped the blankets of their legs and were kicking every ball, no doubt trying to "Give it to Dixie". The noise was such that a Hollywood special effects team would have marvelled at it. Suddenly, the decibel counter flew into the air as Gray scored to put us 2-1 ahead. Boy, this was what we had been waiting for all those years - our first European final was in touching distance if we could just keep Bayern at bay.

The Germans were desperately going for another away goal, which would take them through. Then, the gods hushed as Steven picked the ball up somewhere near the centre circle, glided towards their penalty area and let fly. The ball hit the back of the net. The noise from the fans behind the goal sent the roof of the Gwladys Street soaring into the air before miraculously falling back into place. Around the ground there were so many men kissing each other, it looked like a Gay Pride festival. The Germans looked at each other, crestfallen, as from the heavens came the sound of Tchaikovsky's 1812 Overture, with cannons exploding.

21. FINALLY

Rapid Vienna
European Cup Winners Cup
1984-85

It was one of the biggest parties ever held by Merseysiders, with an estimated 25,000 determined to enjoy themselves. The party was in Rotterdam and the occasion was Everton winning their first European trophy. However there was the formality of the game. Before we could be presented with the trophy, we had to go through the motions of the final and make sure that we scored more goals than the other team. The fall guys were Rapid Vienna; it wasn't fair on them. Everton were on a roll; not even a select European XI would have stopped the Blues that night.

It had been a wonderful season. We had already wrapped up the league, winning the championship for the first time since 1970, and with style. It had perhaps upset some sections of the London-based media that we had outpaced Tottenham Hotspur in the title race. But what the heck did we care. We would show everyone how good we were next season when we played in the European Cup.

There was much swapping of scarves and hats between the Evertonians and Viennese, largely conducted in what might be termed "prisoner-of-war film" English. But we were not going to let them con us. "Are you sure this is a Rapid Vienna hat? It says Rapid Wien." It was then I learnt that while we say Vienna, they say Wien. Travel broadens the mind, as they say.

The Rapid Vienna support was thought to be in the region of 15,000, perhaps not that many. But they were not only outnumbered, they were bemused, dumbfounded, perplexed by the Evertonians' pre-match euphoria. The Evertonians were so effervescent, so effusive, that many Rapid fans had a look on their faces which said: "Who are these people? They're off another planet."

Yes, Planet Evertonia. For years, we had largely been off the radar screens but now we were heading back as one of the leading lights in the footballing universe.

It was perhaps wrong to write off Rapid before the game. Austria had been one of Europe's leading football nations. There had been professional football in the country since 1911 and in the 1930s the Austrian national team went 16 matches unbeaten with a technically advanced style of play for the day, becoming known as the "Wunder Team". They reached the semi-finals of the 1934 World Cup, a feat that Austria repeated 20 years later. The Austrian team of the early 50s was so good that in 1953 six Austrian players were considered worthy of selection in a theoretical FIFA World XI, including Ernst Happel who later managed Feyenoord and Hamburg to European Cup triumphs and Holland to the 1978 World Cup final.

Austrian club football had been dominated by Rapid and their arch-rivals, Austria Vienna. Rapid had not only won the Austrian championship 27 times, but also the German championship in 1941, following Hitler's re-alignment of national boundaries.

But although Austria had made the World Cup quarter-finals in 1978 and 1982, their clubs often sold their best players. A classic example was the Rapid Vienna dangerman in 1985, Hans Krankl. He had returned to Austria after several seasons with Barcelona, with whom he had won the Cup Winners Cup in 1979.

The players' attitude to the game was summed up by Kevin Ratcliffe who wrote in his autobiography: "Games had been coming so thick and fast while we headed for the treble, we just didn't have time to think too long about the importance of them or get nervous. Meeting the Viennese was just another job to be done."

The games had also been coming so thick and fast for supporters who had been struggling to find not only the money for the games, but also the time off work. Among the author's match-going companions at this time was one lad - who shall remain nameless, but I shall call him Paul - who worked offshore on a rig. Once offshore, staff could only get back to dry land if there were extentuating circumstances in which case a helicopter would be summoned. There was one Everton game that season which Paul just did not wish to miss. He arranged that a phone call was made to his offshore workplace, imparting the news that his uncle Bill had died. Paul told his boss he had been very close to his uncle Bill and must go to the funeral. A helicopter was called and landed on the helipad to take Paul. He was just about to put his head down and run to the copter when his boss clutched his arm and said in Paul's ear: "Let's hope they win, eh."

Six weeks later, Paul was at a family gathering when he was suddenly given a dressing down by his furious cousin, whom we shall call Anne. She bawled at him: "I'm disgusted with you, Paul. I thought you were a decent man. How can you say such a thing as that my dad died in an accident, when he hadn't, just so you can go and watch bloody Everton?"

Paul replied calmly: "I'm sorry, Anne. But if there had been a replay, you were next."

Fortunately, Paul was onshore on the day of the Cup Winners Cup final - Wednesday 15 May - and took one of the many flights from Liverpool airport. Some of us had travelled over on the Sunday for aperitifs in Amsterdam. Eight of us met in Rotterdam on the day of the game, including Alan with his white stick. The city centre was awash with Evertonians, overflowing from bars. Everyone has their own tale to tell. We decided to go off the beaten track and wandered into a bar frequented by middle-aged Dutchmen. I cannot remember the name of the place but I know it wasn't "The Clog and Tulips". Conversation was struck up, rounds of beers exchanged and when we decided to leave for the game an hour and a half later they presented us with a painting that was hanging on the wall. Alan had it hanging on his wall at home until he passed away in 1999.

Inside the ground was a kaleidoscope of blue and white flags, scarves and shirts. As soon as the game started, Evertonians expected a goal but it did not materialise, not in the first-half anyway. Strangely it was 0-0 at half-time.

Ten years later Neville Southall said: "All I remember of the 1985 final was the flares before the game. I know it sounds daft but it was a non-event in lots of ways because everyone knew we were going to win. We had beaten the best side in the competition, Bayern Munich, in the semi-finals. That was our final. And the second leg, when we beat them on a memorable night at Goodison, will always stand out. But after that it was just a formality. The final was just one of those games you knew you were going to win."

Ratcliffe later admitted to a degree of anxiety when it was still goalless at half time despite Everton having had most of the play.

But in the dressing room Howard Kendall assured them that the goals would come if they kept on playing their normal game.

Little more than 10 minutes into the second half, Andy Gray struck a volley that flew into the net.

Trevor Steven struck the second at the back post from a corner by Kevin Sheedy. We were coasting, 2-0 up, but then Krankl scored to pull one back. We weren't going to throw it away, were we? No need to worry. Just a couple of minutes later, Sheedy scored with a shot from outside the box. When the final whistle went, with the score 3-1, there was a huge outpouring of joy as Evertonians hugged each other, danced and sang.

It had taken us 23 years to finally win a European trophy and the feeling was one of pure joy. The 1984-85 season was a particularly enjoyable time for those of us who were aged in our late 20s, single, with money to spend on great nights out and watching Everton, who were at their best. Bruce Springsteen had just written a song which summed it all up, Glory Days. "Well they'll pass you by, glory days, in the wink of a young girl's eye."

It would only be two weeks before a terrible shadow fell over our European success. Liverpool went to Brussels to play Juventus in the European Cup final. There was trouble at one end of the dilapidated Heysel stadium, it resulted in a crush and 39 people died, nearly all from Italy. As a result, English clubs were banned from the European tournaments, stopping Everton from going out to win the 1986 European Cup.

Of course, the ban was absolutely nothing, a mere triviality, compared to the deaths of 39 people whose lives were cut short and the grief of their loved ones. But any history of Everton Football Club must note that the ban was a significant blow to the development of the club. Many Blues feel that a ban on Everton was unjust. As has been said before: "There is a football match that has nothing to do with us, there is trouble there and we get banned from Europe. How do you explain that?"

If trouble with football crowds had been previously unknown, it is likely that only Liverpool would have been banned. But violence at and around football grounds was all too common in England in the Seventies and early Eighties. The supporters of various English clubs had also exported it to Europe. Notable examples were the riots involving Leeds supporters in Paris at the 1975 European Cup Final and Tottenham supporters in Rotterdam in 1974. Boorish supporters of the England football team had also been responsible for violence abroad.

Mainland Europeans were sick of it and the British Government was fed up with the country's reputation being tarnished. The Prime Minister in 1985 was Margaret Thatcher who had little, if any, enthusiasm for football. To her, the game was something that merely caused problems, particularly in spring 1985. TV viewers worldwide had seen a violent pitch invasion by Millwall fans at Luton; fighting between followers of Birmingham and Leeds had led to a wall crumbling, crushing a teenager; but worst of all in England, there was a fire in a stand at a game between Bradford and Lincoln and 56 people died. Now came this tragedy in Belgium, which was captured on television and shown around the world.

A few days after the Heysel tragedy, Football Association chiefs went to 10 Downing Street for a meeting then stood outside and announced that it was banning all English clubs from playing in Europe. UEFA chiefs – reeling not only from the tragedy but also from the fierce criticism of their arrangements at Heysel – later banned English clubs from Europe indefinitely, with the period provisionally set at five years, with an extra three for Liverpool. It has been reported that Everton went to court and appealed, but lost.

It was so, so, so frustrating because we had one of our greatest ever teams. But to really make our mark in the history books we needed to win the European Cup. We had looked at the other clubs due to compete in the tournament in 1985-86 and there was nobody for us to fear. This was borne out by the 1986 European Cup final, won by Steaua Bucharest on penalties - and most of them were missed - after two hours of goalless, almost soulless, football against a Barcelona team managed by Terry Venables.

Consider the views of Gary Lineker, who had one season at Everton before joining Barcelona. Writing in the Sunday Telegraph, he said: "Everton were at the peak of their powers when I joined them in 1985. They were not only the best side I ever played for but also the best around. They had great quality, terrific team spirit, an exceptional defence and the ability to both create and score goals."

The ban on English clubs in Europe was something we had to reluctantly accept. I remember thinking at the time that a good chunk of luck would be required to bounce back from it. We would need to win a trophy, preferably the championship, in the year that English clubs were allowed back. This required fortuitous timing. Rather than tread water at the top of English football then dip below the surface just before the ban was lifted, which is largely what we did, it would be better to first dip for a while then surge back to the top just as the ban was lifted. But the 1985 team was far too good to finish mid-table the next season.

Of course, the ideal would have been to stay at the top of English football for five years or so. However in 1990 the players who had been aged in their early to mid-20s in Rotterdam were now all approaching the age of 30, or were older.

In May 1990, Liverpool won the league, with Aston Villa in second place, while Manchester United won the FA Cup. In July 1990, UEFA chiefs met in Geneva to consider a report from British Sports Minister Colin Moynihan which recommended that Villa and United should be allowed to play in Europe in the following season. A plea for Liverpool was not made, presumably because of their longer ban. UEFA agreed that English clubs should be let back in, but warned that if there was more trouble, the ban would be re-imposed. Villa would play in the UEFA Cup and United in the Cup Winners Cup.

Many Blues fans felt that if Liverpool could not enter the European Cup, then another English club should - and that club should be Everton because we had been denied entry in 1985. Everton had finished sixth in 1990 so the Blues would have sent a reasonably strong team. There was a precedent of sorts. In 1958 Wolves entered the European Cup as champions, but an invitation was also extended to Manchester United who had been knocked out in the previous tournament's semi-finals following the Munich tragedy. But we were to receive no special treatment.

Then one year later, new UEFA president Lennart Johansson said in an interview before an UEFA executive committee meeting in London in 1991: "I want to see Liverpool back. I think Liverpool have suffered enough now and we must not forget that six years ago, so-called supporters were given the chance to cause trouble by bad organisation. We must remember that Liverpool didn't try to defend themselves, fully accepted their punishment, have done the utmost to help and that we have not received any reports of trouble since."

Johansson was probably right in everything he said about Liverpool, who went on to take part in the 1991-92 UEFA Cup. It is worth remembering that the vast majority of Reds fans at Heysel were totally blameless. But where was the concern for Everton? With Liverpool's impressive record in Europe, I do wonder if Johansson & Co felt that European competitions were a little devalued without the Reds. It is ironic that after the ban on English clubs was imposed, Liverpool would spend six years out of Europe, but Everton would be out for ten.

But could we have dealt better with the ban? In 1986, should we have rejected Barcelona's £2.75million offer for Gary Lineker who scored 30 league goals in his one season with us? We won the title the following season without the striker we had bought for £850,000, but how good it would have been to be able to bank on his goals for the next few seasons. Could we have done more to keep Howard Kendall in the manager's seat, which he vacated in 1987 to take over at Athletic Bilbao?

There is also an historic Everton failure to consider. We have never retained a major trophy. Not once have Everton won the championship or FA Cup two seasons in succession. It looked as if we would retain the championship in 1986 but we were pipped at the post and finished second.

In the years that followed, some Evertonians would sometimes be accused of having a "bitter" attitude towards Liverpool. Certainly the ban was a sore point. Possibly the longer we went without success in the Premiership, the more we looked back to the ban. And possibly the more Champions League games were broadcast live on TV, the more we sat at home, wondering what might have been. Springsteen's lyrics in Glory Days were perhaps prophetic: "I hope when I get old I don't sit around thinking about it, but I probably will."

Sadly, this issue has become a source of antagonism between Everton and Liverpool supporters. This may persist unless there is some give and take on both sides, with everybody remembering that it is just a game.

It would help if Reds could accept that we had a wonderful team in 1985 and were denied, through no fault of our own, a great opportunity to go all the way in the European Cup the following season, and reap the financial benefits that would have followed, putting us in a stronger monetary position in subsequent seasons. And if the Reds would stop asking that tedious Eurovision Song Contest question, especially as they know it doesn't bring out the best in us.

It would help if Blues would remember that the vast majority of Reds fans at Heysel were totally blameless, and if they would refrain from "that chant" at derby matches. While the UEFA ban was a major setback to Everton FC, it was far from being the cause of all our problems over the next 20 years.

It would be good if there was a game at Goodison or Anfield where Blues and Reds could sit together again, un-segregated. In 1964 there was a testimonial match for Dixie Dean. It was the two clubs' English players against the two clubs' Scottish players. And so Alex Young and Ian St John lined up together.

What about a game involving the clubs' British players against their overseas players? A team featuring Duncan Ferguson and Steven Gerrard lining up against one involving Mikel Arteta and Fernando Morientes. David Moyes could referee the first half and Rafael Benitez the second half, so we could see how good Premiership managers are at refereeing.

22. A CHILL WIND

Reykjavik
European Cup Winners Cup
1995-96

After 10 years in the cold, we were finally allowed back into European competition after winning the FA Cup in 1995. And what did the draw give us? A game in the cold, up in Iceland.

Still, we were delighted to be back. It had been a difficult 10 years. First there had been the European ban, then the decline in the health of the club's major shareholder which came at a most unfortunate time.

England's top clubs had to think long and hard about how best to contend with the exclusion from Europe. Strategic decisions needed to be taken. Should a club join a breakaway league? How far should it go down the road of live televising of games? Redevelop the ground or build a new one elsewhere? These were challenging business questions which Sir John Moores would have loved to tackle in his prime. But as these questions arose, he was approaching his 90th birthday which he celebrated in January 1987.

Obviously he was not as fit and agile as he had been. Merely attending meetings at this age would be physically demanding. However he had put in place trusted lieutenants.

Since 1960, Moores had drafted on to the Everton board men who had impressed him with their work for Littlewoods. Before Sir Philip Carter, who was knighted in 1991, there were the likes of Gordon Watts and Holland Hughes. While Watts was a Littlewoods executive, Hughes was a lawyer with a Merseyside law firm who had represented Littlewoods in their negotiations with the Football League.

Littlewoods men were placed in key positions at Everton throughout Moores' reign. Brian West, Littlewoods public relations adviser, edited the programme and handled the club's public relations at the time of its centenary in 1978.

The relationship between Littlewoods and Everton became even more apparent in 1987 when Desmond Pitcher became a director in the Goodison boardroom. Pitcher, Littlewoods chief executive since 1983, was to become Everton's deputy chairman in 1990. Then, with Carter still chairman, it meant that the two top boardroom positions were taken by Littlewoods men. They had a lot on their plate.

At Goodison attendances dipped to an average of around 25,000 by 1990 even though the team had finished sixth. The ground was looking in need of a makeover. The terracing directly underneath the Park End stand was closed off. Negotiations over the live televising of league games were shortly to end in the deal to kick off the Premiership in 1992. But even though football was becoming more fashionable following Gazza's tears at Italia '90, our average attendance in the first Premiership season was down to just over 20,000.

Pitcher had even more to contend with at Littlewoods, described in the Sunday Times in February 1990 as "Britain's biggest and most secretive private company". Journalists Philip Beresford and Chris

Blackhurst wrote a feature that painted a picture of the Moores being "a family at war", with particular tension between brothers Peter and John junior. Apparently this had simmered for some time, but did not matter so much when their father was healthy. But now Sir John was frail and infirm.

Littlewoods, worth more than £1.6billion according to some reports, was still totally owned by the Moores family. The three arms of the empire - pools, mail order and retail - were facing increasing competition. What policies should Littlewoods adopt? "The family remains deeply divided over flotation while Littlewoods' executives are thought to favour the idea," wrote Beresford and Blackhurst.

Flotation meant floating the company on the stock market, letting anybody buy shares in Littlewoods. This would have enabled the 30 to 40 family members who owned a share of the company to turn it into cash, mountains of cash. "Family members are reluctant to discuss publicly what they regard as an intensely personal affair," wrote Beresford and Blackhurst.

But the two journalists had their sources and told how John junior's children - he had eight - had for the last 12 months "been holding shareholder meetings in their houses dotted around Britain on a monthly and even a weekly basis".

Matters were brought to a head by Sir John's state of health. In 1989 a burglar had broken into his home. According to press reports, Sir John was attacked and never fully recovered. Subsequently, if there was any mention of the great man, he was said to be in poor health, frail, infirm or living quietly. More suggestive was a quote attributed to a source by Beresford and Blackhurst in their Sunday Times article: "If only Sir John could have 24 hours of lucidity...."

Of course, the club's very able directors could make decisions, tough decisions. But regards any thoughts of re-financing the club, such as the issue of new shares, little could be done without the approval of the major owner, or trustees he had appointed. It was far from an ideal situation.

Howard Kendall had returned to the club and was manager in our first season in the Premiership. With attendances for some games at Goodison down to the 18,000 mark, it should not have been surprising that the club sold Martin Keown two-thirds the way through the season to Arsenal for £2million.

At the end of the season, in May 1993, Ken Rogers of the Liverpool Echo reported that the Moores family had instructed merchant bankers Hill Samuel to investigate ways of re-financing the club. "A buy-out of their stake is seen as the most straight-forward option," said David Walker in the Daily Mail.

The club played the reports with a straight bat, saying they were of "a highly speculative nature". Chairman David Marsh issued a statement which read: "I am authorised by the major shareholder to say that he has no intention of selling his shareholding."

With the club reported to be £4million in debt, on a turnover of around £8million, Peter Jardine of the Daily Post interviewed Marsh who told him: "There are 2,500 shares and Sir John Moores has the major holding of these. He is 97 and poorly and his interests are being looked after by trustees. But he is not going to sell those shares so you have to look at other ways of getting finance into the club."

The board was trying its best in trying circumstances to move the club forward. In October 1993 it emerged that plans had been drawn up for a new stand at the Park End. It would cost £2.5m but

£1.3million would be covered by a grant from the Football Trust. However the stand, with around 7,000 seats, was little bigger than Tranmere's Kop stand. Critics would later argue that a bigger, two-tier structure should have been built. But of course it had to be paid for.

Liverpool were better placed than Everton to withstand the financial consequences of the UEFA ban. Basically, they had enjoyed a golden period in Europe and, as a result, had become a worldwide brand. Between 1976 and 1984, Liverpool won the championship seven times and the European Cup four times. It was a phenomenal run. A lot of their triumphs were televised and a lot of football fans - especially children - not only around Britain, but throughout Europe and across the world, declared themselves to be Liverpool fans.

When the 1990s came, many of those children were young adults, the main targets of the marketing men encircling the game. Increasingly, the major companies saw the Premiership as a nice way to market themselves and so they offered lucrative sponsorship deals to the clubs with the highest profiles and biggest number of followers.

In the 1990s, Liverpool only won three trophies but their annual revenue went from £4.8million in 1989 to £17.3million in 1994. Over the same period, Everton's annual revenue went from £5.8million to £8.9million - figures taken from Winners & Losers, The Business Strategy of Football, by Stefan Szymanski and Tim Kuypers.

Meanwhile in November 1993, David Prentice of the Echo printed a table which showed that since taking over three years earlier, Kendall had spent £7.95million on players and recouped £7.85million in sales. A few weeks later Kendall wanted to spend

£1.5million on buying centre forward Dion Dublin but he was unable to do so. On Saturday 4th December, 1993, just 13,677 fans turned up at Goodison to see Everton beat Southampton 1-0 to go 11th in the table. Little more than an hour later, Kendall resigned.

There was an outcry among fans at what was perceived as the board's "stinginess". It must have been a great honour for Marsh, a Kirkby GP, when he became club chairman but unfortunately he is remembered in Everton folklore as the man who told Kendall he could not buy Dion Dublin. But Marsh would not have taken such a decision on his own. Also on the board were Littlewoods duo Pitcher and Carter, the Lord Lieutenant of Merseyside Alan Waterworth, West End impresario Bill Kenwright, Keith Tamlin and David Newton.

Marsh should have been given a medal for being chairman in possibly the most difficult time in the club's history. Because around 10 weeks before Kendall quit, Sir John Moores had died in September 1993, at the age of 97.

Now the issue of succession was to the fore. None of Sir John's children had sufficient interest in Everton to want to take over, otherwise they would have done so, possibly even years earlier. But why should they? All four were all adults before their father took an active role in the club. Prior to that, they had all been to schools miles away from Merseyside. The sons, John junior and Peter, had returned to live on Merseyside and would have had an affection for the club, but they had other interests. For instance, Peter felt about opera the same way that an Everton season ticket holder feels about the Blues. Each to their own.

There was one family member however who was an exception to this rule, Cecil's son David. For whatever reasons, he was a passionate football fan but he was a Red, a rather committed one.

I suspect that as a boy he was brought up to watch both clubs but that he was later won over to the Red cause by the Kop factor and the Shankly charisma.

Cecil Moores died in 1989. The following year, son David became a director at Anfield. Then in August 1991 he became Liverpool chairman. The rapidity of his rise was reminiscent of the way his uncle John had become chairman of Everton just three months after becoming a director. In 1994, David was heavily involved in a rights issue at Liverpool that raised £9million for stadium development, with Moores reportedly putting in most of it.

In 1994, after more than 30 years in the hands of the Moores family, control of Everton passed into the hands of Peter Johnson. He had taken over Tranmere when they looked likely to crash out of the Football League. He appointed a brilliant manager, a former Everton player, Johnny King, and the Rovers rose to within touching distance of the Premiership, only failing in the play-offs.

When Everton won the FA Cup in 1995 in Johnson's first season as chairman, it seemed he had the Midas touch. We were back in Europe and had splashed out on a string of internationals.

There was some disappointment among Evertonians that we should be drawn to play a team on a more northerly island - or, let's not beat about the bush, a club from a country where the beer was so expensive. As the team prepared to set off for Iceland, the first person tnat journalists sought out for some quotes was Neville Southall, the only survivor from the Cup Winners Cup final.

Southall, aged 37, told of his conviction that Everton would have gone on to greater success in the mid-80s but for the ban on English clubs. "We would have frightened Europe to death the next season but suddenly it was out of our hands," he said. "Everton should be world renowned by now and if we'd stayed in Europe we would be."

Manager Joe Royle had to contend with a UEFA rule that there should be no more than three players in a team from a country different to the one in which the club was located. Royle had six non-English players: Southall and Barry Horne of Wales, Sweden's Anders Limpar, Nigerian Daniel Amokachi, the Ukrainian Andrei Kanchelskis who had played for Russia, and Duncan Ferguson of Scotland. Foreign-born players could become "assimilated" to the country in which their club was based. However this did not apply to any of Everton's players, even Horne and Southall who were born and bred little more than an hour's drive from Goodison Park.

Kanchelskis, who had a dislocated shoulder, and Ferguson were out anyway. That left one man for Royle to drop. He chose Horne, the boyhood Blue. Royle said: "I feel desperately sorry for Barry. He's been terrific this season, right up there with our best players, and I've apologised for leaving him behind. I've told him it won't be this way every time. Barry's got vast experience abroad with Wales, as he was quick to point out, but it's the balance of the squad in the end.'

Reykjavik were emerging from a long slump, which was out of keeping with a long and successful history in Icelandic football, littered with firsts. The first football club in Iceland, Knattspyrnufélag Reykjavíkur - to give the club its full name – was formed in 1899 after a Scottish printer working in Iceland had introduced the game to his new friends. Usually known in Iceland as KR, and in English as Reykjavik, they were, in 1912, the first to win the Icelandic championship - after defeating the two other clubs. Yes, at first, there were only three in the league.

When the first division was played on a home and away basis for the first time, in 1959, KR won every game, scoring 41 and conceding only six in 10 matches. The next season they won the first Cup Final in Iceland, defeating Fram 2-0. They followed this up in 1961 by becoming the first to do the double in Iceland. In 1968 they won the Icelandic title for the 20th time but it was to be another 31 years before they landed the championship again, even though they tried a variety of managers, most notably in 1985 when they appointed Gordon Lee. The former Everton boss spent three years at the club. As at Goodison, Lee's team challenged for the championship but fell away in the final stages.

The change in fortune came in 1994 when the club appointed Gudjón Thórdarson who had been manager of arch rivals ÍA. In 1995 KR finished second in the league but beat Fram 2-0 in the Cup final to clinch the club's first major trophy in 26 years.

Shortly before meeting Everton, KR won their first ever game in Europe. It was the 10th time they had qualified but they had always been knocked out straight away. Put into the qualifying round of the Cup Winners Cup, KR beat Grevenmacher from Luxembourg.

The typical attendance for a KR home game was around 2,000. But 6,000 crammed in for the visit of the English cup winners, expecting to see goals. In KR Reykjavik's previous ties with British clubs - Liverpool, Aberdeen and Queens Park Rangers - Reykjavik had scored two and conceded 32.
Perhaps the gap in quality between Icelandic and British football was starting to narrow, or perhaps Everton were just off form. But our game there was a close game, only settled in the dying minutes.

For if Everton's very first game in European football, against Dunfermline, was a disappointment, so was their return after the

Heysel ban. The Blues turned in a ragged display against Reykjavik whose team were mainly part-timers. Their main threat was the Croat striker Mihajlo Bibercic, a full-time professional.

Horne's place was taken by John Ebbrell who was one of Everton's best performers. After hitting the bar in the opening minutes, Ebbrell scored midway through the first half when, following a powerful run by Amokachi, he latched on to a loose ball in the Icelandic penalty box and poked it in the net.

It was a nice moment for Ebbrell, whose contribution to Everton in the Nineties was frequently under-estimated. After graduating from the FA's much-hyped School of Excellence, he was burdened with the mantle of being the club's next great young hope. A combative midfield player, nobody went in for more 50-50 tackles on Everton's behalf in the Nineties than Ebbrell. Probably his only rival on that score would be Dave Watson. But if you agree that a central midfielder makes more 50-50 tackles in a game than a centre half who spends much of the game standing directly behind his main opponent, the award would have to go to Ebbrell. He had had the honour of captaining the England under-21 team. But, just like Fred Pickering three decades earlier, he had suffered the heartache of not being picked to play in the FA Cup final. As a result he was on the transfer list at the time of the Reykjavik game

The Icelandic team were responding valiantly to the roaring support of their biggest crowd in years. Bibercic volleyed a loose ball against the crossbar, then moments later coolly fired home Reykjavik's 38th-minute equaliser from the penalty spot after Unsworth brought down Heimir Gudjonsson on the by-line. It was 1-1 at half-time with the home supporters in 6,000 crowd delighted to see their team holding their own.

There were to be another two penalties in the game. In the 57th minute Hinchcliffe was brought down by Steinar Adolfsson and

Unsworth sent Finnbogason the wrong way to make it 2-1. But within 10 minutes the Icelandic team was level. Gudmundur Benediktsson was brought down and Bibercic sent Southall the wrong way again. Finnbogason made a string of second-half saves to deny Hinchcliffe, Rideout and Amokachi. But he could do nothing to stop Amo's late blast. With just three minutes to go, Amokachi swivelled on the edge of the area and fired home to make it 3-2 to Everton. Thankfully, this time the Blues were not required to hang on to their lead for too long.

After the game, Thordarson said: "I'm proud of my players tonight and they are all very disappointed they did not win. The only difference was that Everton had the luck. Amokachi hit a fantastic goal but we hit the bar twice. We gave Everton problems because they are too square at the back and they will struggle against better sides in Europe."

Royle said: "I never felt we were in danger of losing. We've got three away goals for the second leg, which is a bonus. It was a strange performance but we got there in the end. They were always going to rise to the occasion and some of their players did really well. We probably missed a bit of Barry Horne's authority in midfield and young Matt Jackson was struggling for match fitness."

Everton then had three away games and failed to win one, losing 3-2 to Nottingham Forest, drawing at Millwall in the League Cup, and a 2-1 defeat at West Ham.

In the second leg against Reykjavik, Craig Short, a £2.7m summer signing from Derby, was making his home debut. However the visitors took the lead in the 20th minute when Bibercic set up Einar Por Danielsson who ran on and shot low past Southall. The visitors could easily have gone in at halftime ahead on aggregate. Benediktsson, 25 yards out, hit a shot that took a deflecion off Unsworth and Southall had to fling himself to his right to stop the visitors scoring again.

With the score 1-0 on the night and 3-3 on aggregate, Everton went in at the interval to a chorus of boos from a disappointing, and disappointed, crowd of 18,000. It seemed that Icelandic teams did not bring the best out of Everton at Goodison.

The players were more concerned however about Amokachi. In the 36th minute "Amo" clashed heads with Reykjavik's Pormodur Egilsson in a challenge for a high ball and lay prone. He had been taken semi-conscious for brain scans to the neurological unit at nearby Walton Hospital.

Everton needed a goal to re-assert their authority but it did not come until the 57th minute when Stuart, on as substitute for Amokachi, ran on to a Rideout header and hit a shot which deflected off defender Egilsson and over keeper Finnbogason.

In the 66th minute, 20-year-old Tony Grant scored his first goal for Everton with a right-foot shot from 16 yards. It took the pressure off, putting Everton 2-1 up on the night and 5-3 on aggregate. Two minutes from the end, after an incisive run and pass by John Ebbrell, Rideout scored from close range to make it 3-1 on the night. After the game, the win was overshadowed in the Everton dressing room by concern for Amokachi. But he made a full recovery.

23. KURSE OF KOEMAN

Feyenoord
European Cup Winners Cup
1995-96

It was the first time the Blues had been pitted against a club they had played before in European competition. With Rotterdam having been the scene of our Cup Winners Cup triumph of 85, the media tended to portray it more as a return to a happy hunting ground. But older Evertonians were also mindful of that defeat in the Kuip stadium in 1980.

As the first leg in Rotterdam approached, Peter Johnson was still in the honeymoon phase of his five-year reign at Goodison which formally began in July 1994. He was to become a controversial figure but his reign started brightly.

He had been a butcher's boy who had started a sideline, taking regular payments from customers then at the end of the year presenting them with a Christmas hamper. Apparently John and Cecil Moores had started their mail order business in a similar way, taking regular payments until a customer had enough to make a purchase. Johnson had floated his company Park Foods on the stock exchange, making him a very rich man.

A keen football fan, he had been a season ticket holder at Anfield. This was later to be used in evidence against him, especially after we ran into trouble during his reign and a banner appeared on the Kop, saying, "Agent Johnson, Mission Accomplished."

But Johnson very much wanted Everton to be successful, I have no doubt, for reasons of pride and finance. Have you ever noticed how so many self-made man cannot sit still and just enjoy their riches? They are driven men who are always looking for the next challenge.

Let's give Johnson some credit. I believe he re-invigorated the club. In 1993-94 the average attendance was less than 23,000. Only three league games attracted more than 27,000 - Liverpool, Manchester United and Wimbledon. But the following season, with new optimism under Johnson, the average gate was more than 31,000, rising to more than 35,000 the following season.

Of course, this was not all down to Johnson. There was also that memorable day - Saturday 7 May, 1994 - when a revivalist rally was held at Goodison Park. Well, that's the only way I can describe the atmosphere. To avoid relegation, we needed a win against a Wimbledon team portrayed as the meanest in the league. Attendances that season at Goodison had been as low as 13,000 for a league game and, under manager Mike Walker, we had slowly slithered down the table.

A lot of Evertonians had stopped going to Goodison, or went less often. The lads who were still going week in, week out, felt a need to round up the lads, Blues Brothers style, for one big reunion. Elwood from Childwall and Jake from Walton jumped in their Chevrolet and drove round the streets of Liverpool, knocking on doors: "Eh, come on, remember all those gigs we used to do, all the towns we used to visit, all the good times we had. Remember

Rotterdam. Well, we've got to get together one more time. It's to save the club. We need you on Saturday, you've got to be there!"

It was a lock-out and one of the most bizarre games ever played at Goodison. For one thing, the Park End was a building site. But on three sides of the crowd was a baying mob of Blues brothers, including Alan Wynne. That Wimbledon team prided themselves on being hard, but they almost tip-toed on to the pitch. However they took a 2-0 lead. Thankfully, the Everton players did not give up, nor did the crowd who sang and shouted for Everton with all the fire and brimstone of a revivalist rally. We won 3-2, thanks partly to that outburst of Evertonianism that was to spill over into the following season.

The fervour from that remarkable afternoon, coupled with £25million injected into the club under Johnson, gave Everton a new lease of life.

The investment was in two tranches. Before he came to the club, there were 2,500 shares in the club. As part of the takeover deal, there was a rights issue in which another 2,500 shares were created, for which Johnson paid £4,000 each, thus injecting £10million into the club. Two years later there was an issue of a further 30,000 shares in which existing shareholders were given the chance to buy another six shares at £500 each for every one they held. Johnson underwrote this issue, promising to buy any shares that were not bought by existing holders. It resulted in the number of shares rising from 5,000 to 35,000 and a cash injection of £15million. It was these issues of new shares that financed the purchases of internationals such as Andrei Kanchelskis, Duncan Ferguson, Daniel Amokachi and Nick Barmby.

Like Moores before him, Johnson also tried to boost the club's all-round efficiency and commercial viability, for example, building a much larger souvenir store. Another similarity was that on becoming an all-powerful chairman he allowed the manager he inherited, Mike Walker, to spend large sums of money on players then sacked him within a year and brought in a former Everton centre forward, Joe Royle. In Moores' case, the names were Johnny Carey and Harry Catterick.

Johnson was bold enough to suggest that Everton needed to move away from Goodison Park and build a new stadium, complete with prawn sandwich boxes (corporate entertainment facilities). Among Evertonians today, this matter still causes a huge clash - should we stay or should we go now - but it is a debate crucial to the club's future, and one that Johnson instigated.

Our FA Cup triumph in 1995 had been a great boost to Evertonians who had consoled the Manchester United supporters at Wembley with a rousing rendition of Always Look On The Bright Side Of Life. It would be another great step for Everton if we could have a good run in Europe, Our second round opponents, Feyenoord, had just won the Dutch Cup for the fourth time in five years. Strangely they would not win it for at least another 10 years.

The first leg at Goodison was a game preceded by some interesting remarks from Ronald Koeman, who had joined Feyenoord after a glorious spell at Barcelona. He said: "We always feel we have a sporting chance against the English because they don't stick to what they know. They feel compelled to play a more continental game. They change their system and it causes them problems. They rarely play to their strengths."

His comments were portrayed as taunts but in the light of Everton's lack of success in Europe - and England's too - they offer substantial food for thought. Seeking a riposte, the press turned to Paul Rideout who replied: "Koeman is a quality player and it is always an interesting challenge to play against someone of that calibre. But he is slow these days and that is something we have been working on and we have been told we have got to get at him."

Koeman was 32 and coming to the end of a fantastic playing career. After being spotted at FC Groningen, the young centre half spent three years at Ajax, three at PSV Eindhoven, during which they won the 1988 European Cup, before spending six seasons at Barcelona in which time they won four successive Spanish titles and the 1992 European Cup when he scored the only goal in the final. He was the first player to win the European Cup with two different clubs. But it was his reputation as a free kick specialist that brought him most fame. He was a defender with a goalscoring record the envy of most forwards. In 192 league matches for Barcelona, he scored 67 goals, the majority from dead ball situations. Koeman had also been one of the stars in Holland's 1988 European Championship winning side.

But Koeman was unpopular with England football fans. He was seen as an opponent who had unfairly denied England a place in the 1994 World Cup finals. In a crucial qualifier in Rotterdam, Koeman had committed a professional foul on England's David Platt as he bore down on goal. Television replays showed Platt had been brought down inside the box, but the referee awarded a free-kick outside, which England failed to score from, and Koeman was shown only a yellow card, not a red. Later in the game Koeman put Holland in the lead with a re-taken free-kick and they went on to win 2-0.

Feyenoord were playing their first game under new coach, Arie Haan, and Rideout warned against the "Joe Royle effect". He said: "We have to be aware of the fact they've got a new manager because it was proved perfectly here last season that when a new man comes in, it can lift players."

Royle was pre-occupied with problems in his own ranks because his squad was ravaged by not only injuries and ineligibility but also imprisonment and a long-distance international call-up. Duncan Ferguson was serving the jail sentence imposed on him for headbutting an opposing player in a game during his Rangers career. Daniel Amokachi had been ordered by Nigeria to go to Uzbekistan for an Afro-Asian Cup clash, while Ukrainian Andrei Kanchelskis was ineligible.

Following the Reykjavik game, Everton had lost at home to Newcastle in the Premiership and Millwall in the Coca-Cola Cup then drawn at Bolton. They had won only two out of their first nine league games. Royle recalled Anders Limpar and the recently capped England defender David Unsworth. More surprising was the selection of transfer-seeking Vinny Samways. It was his first Goodison Park start for 12 months, and his first at home under Royle.

The game was to be yet another European tie at Goodison in which the Blues failed to turn long periods of domination and possession into goals. And again, they had their keeper to thank for saving them. As early as the fourth minute, Southall made an excellent save. Michael Edirin Obiku turned Gary Ablett on the edge of the Everton area and sent in a right-foot drive destined for the bottom corner until Southall dived to his left.

After that early shock, the Blues largely controlled the first half, with Samways prominent. The Londoner forced several fine saves from Dutch keeper Ed de Goey who had also kept out a close-range effort from Rideout in the eighth minute. An indication of Everton's dominance was that Feyenoord did not win one corner in the first half.

After the break, Samways continued to impress and Limpar came into the game more. But as the second half wore on, Feyenoord came out of their shell. Little had been seen of the set-piece expertise of Koeman but when Feyenoord got a free kick 30 yards out on the hour mark, he strode up to take it. There was an air of anticipation then the sound of jeers when he ballooned it into the stand. But Feyenoord came more and more into the game and twice nearly snatched a win. Ablett cleared an effort off the line and Southall saved brilliantly from Rob Witschge. The game ended 0-0.

Royle put a brave face on the scoreline. "It was a terrific performance," he said. "We still have a great chance over there and I fancy us to get through. A 0-0 draw is far better than a 1-1 result in Europe. Remember, that is Feyenoord's best team whereas we have got players to come back. We will certainly have more pace available for the second leg with people like Daniel Amokachi and Andy Hinchcliffe to come in. I've seen Feyenoord three or four times now and while they are a decent side we've got nothing to be scared of."

When Everton flew to Rotterdam for the second leg, Royle still had selection problems. Already without Ferguson and Kanchelskis, injuries ruled out Samways and Unsworth and cast a doubt over Limpar. Royle also had to bear in mind the three-foreigner rule, if he had three fit foreigners.

As Evertonians gathered in Rotterdam, Royle said: "We're just looking to get the break that will turn things for us. We're not playing desperately badly. We don't leak goals profusely, although we are missing more chances than most. Feyenoord will have to be more adventurous on their own ground. They left out one or two attacking players over here but they will have to be more positive now."

Everton gave a stirring display. After only seven minutes the Blues nearly took the lead when Andy Hinchcliffe's free-kick found defender Short unmarked 10 yards out but Ulrich van Gobbel hurled himself into the path of his shot. The team was skippered by Barry Horne and he drove the Blues on as they outplayed the home side for long spells. Amokachi caused problems up front, notably for De Goey who needed treatment for a bloodied nose in the 20th minute after an aerial clash with the powerfully built Nigerian.

The fact that Everton were playing so well made it all the more heartbreaking when the home side took the lead six minutes before the interval. Henrik Larsson released Tomek Iwan on Everton's left and he set up Obiku just five yards out, but he hit the woodwork. John Ebbrell went to clear but the ball fell to Blinker who shot past Southall from 12 yards.

In the second half, Everton continued in search of their first goal in four games against Feyenoord. But de Goey produced a superb fingertip save to deny Graham Stuart while Rideout neatly created an opening for himself but shot narrowly wide. As the game entered the third quarter, Royle made a bold double substitution, bringing on Tony Grant and Stuart Barlow for Ebbrell and Stuart. Minutes later, a cross from Matt Jackson resulted in a volley from Short but it went straight at de Goey. The keeper denied Everton again, tipping over a Hinchcliffe free kick.

The equaliser was eluding Everton and in stoppage time Koeman crashed into Short, producing an angry reaction from Short whose raised arm had Italian referee Marcello Nicchi reaching for his red card.

Short said: "It was ridiculous. I reacted to a dreadful tackle - I could have got my leg broken by the tackle he made. I did swing round with my arm, but I'm not sure if I made contact. But I was angry at the original challenge. I suppose if you raise your arm you can't complain, but I was very upset about his tackle on me."

Royle angrily and sardonically said of the 1-0 defeat which put Everton out of the competition: "It was a night when we needed a break but the closest thing we got to it was when Ronald Koeman nearly broke Craig Short's leg. It was one of the worst tackles I've seen this season. Short has got severe bruising and six-inch marks right down his leg. I don't think you can argue that there was retaliation, but it disappointed me that the perpetrator wasn't booked."

Koeman, who had suggested that Everton should not play the Continental way, said: "I can understand that they are angry, it's normal. But it was a tackle that happens in every match in England. I made a tackle for the ball, nothing more. It is their reaction to a bad result and a bad night for them. Not every referee is like an English referee. He did touch me. He was sent off for retaliation but sometimes in England that is not a problem. English referees are more likely to accept that."

The sad fact was we had now played Feyenoord four times in the UEFA Cup and failed to score a goal against them in three hours of football. The four games had only produced three goals but they all came from the Rotterdam team.

There was to be more European frustration for Everton at the end of the season when we finished sixth, but were denied a UEFA Cup place due to Wimbledon and Spurs fielding reserve teams in the Intertoto Cup. It could only happen to us.

During the season, relations had soured between UEFA and English football chiefs over the Intertoto which had been relaunched in 1995. UEFA was keen to see English teams take part but there was little enthusiasm from Premier League clubs due to the tournament being held in the summer. Under pressure, Sheffield Wednesday, Spurs and Wimbledon entered teams but filled them with reserves and youth team players. UEFA was furious, going to the extent of placing a one-season ban from European competition on the two London clubs, who were seen as the worst offenders. An appeal led to the bans being rescinded and there might not have been a knock-on effect, but Premiership clubs made clear they would not be entering the 1996 Intertoto. Four English clubs had been allowed in the UEFA Cup in 1995-96 and it was thought it would be the same number for 1996-97, but suddenly the number was down to three. Fifth-placed Arsenal squeezed in, but squeezed out were sixth-placed Everton.

At this point, I wondered if we should apply to join another continent. Twice we had been denied entry to the Fairs Cup because of the one-city, one-club rule. Then we were excluded because of the 1985 ban on English clubs. Soon after getting back in, we were kept out because Wimbledon had fielded their youngest wombles. And don't talk about the wars which started in Europe that led to the break-up of our championship teams of 1915 and 1939.

As for the reign of chairman Johnson, the club's spending on players - and perhaps most crucially, their wages - would go too far, putting the club deeply in debt. Johnson also had to contend with pressing problems at his core business, Park Foods, when plans for a new product hit snags. After the sale of Ferguson to Newcastle in November 1998, Johnson came in for fierce and sustained criticism. He stepped down as chairman and it emerged that he was seeking to sell his majority stake. But it was to be another year before a deal was agreed, another year the club spent in limbo. Our early years as a Premiership club were bumpy ones.

24. COLLINA AND HOPKIRK (DECEASED)

Villarreal
European Champions League
2005-06

THE banner read: "1985 and 1987 Qualified, Sorry we're late, Circumstances beyond our control." One of many flags paraded by Evertonians in Villarreal, it cleverly expressed the frustration that still simmered over that Europe ban of 20 years ago.

The ironical tone of the flag dovetailed neatly with the reaction to our appearance in the Champions League. It was as if we were expected to apologise. We had an official invite but there was still a feeling we had gatecrashed the party. "Oh we know that years ago you used to come here quite a lot, but things have, how shall we put it, moved on since then. We've got to know Liverpool so well and it would be a shame if there was no room for them because you are here. Nothing personal, of course. It's just a question of, you know, maintaining standards. You'd be better off at the party down the road, you'd feel much more at home there, the UEFA Cup they call it, the people there are more your type. I'm sure they will make you welcome."

It wasn't our fault that UEFA now let England's fourth-placed team into Europe's premier club competition. In fact, it's a pity they didn't do that in the Sixties. And it was not our fault that nobody had overtaken us as we stumbled through the last 19 league games, picking up only 21 points.

But there was considerable dismay, in some quarters, most notably sections of the media, that we had succeeded in finishing fourth in May 2005 and qualifying for the Champions League. It was as if some looked upon us as chavs who had won the Lottery and were about to move next door to their big, posh house.

There was a Catch 22 here which many failed to recognise. Clubs with the most money would be most likely to have the best players, win the most games, play the most attractive football and do well in Europe. Everton, and others, would like to be one of those clubs but becoming part of that elite without regularly playing in Europe was very difficult.

And some people had forgotten, if they had ever known anything about football pre-Premiership, that we were once part of the footballing aristocracy, but had fallen from grace. We were, in a way, the Lord Brockett of football. If you don't know who he is, you have obviously never watched the TV series I'm An Evertonian, Get Me Out Of Here, in which B-list celebrities are sent to a jungle to watch videos of Everton in the dismal years. Brockett, whose family had made their fortune in brewing in Victorian Liverpool, and was thus presumably a rival of John Houlding, had previously lived in a magnificent mansion, but following a spot of bother over insurance claims on sports cars, he had been jailed. Everton got out of jail on 7th May, 1994 (the Wimbledon game). Brockett got out of jail some years later and found reality TV to be a useful rehabilitation programme.

Although there were four places in the Champions League for English clubs, some assumed that three were reserved for Liverpool,

Manchester United and Arsenal because they had the most star players and the most "supporters", which ensured big television audiences and consequently contentment for the advertisers and sponsors. Also those three were members of G14, which had been set up to "safeguard the general interests of the member clubs". The fourth spot was for a club of the moment and the one which aroused most interest in 2004-05 was Chelsea who had won the championship with monopoly money to spare.

If the G14 continues without Everton, may I suggest that we should form a rival organisation, called the M62 or A41, and invite other clubs considered by neutrals to be in the shadow of tbeir neighbours, such as Atletico Madrid, Espanyol, Manchester City, TSV Munich 1860 and RSVP Eindhoven.

But when the Premiership season finished in May 2005, Liverpool had not made the cut for the Champions League. For only the fourth time in 40 years, we had finished above them. Weh-hey! What joy we had that season from simply opening a newspaper and just staring non-stop at the Premiership table; my personal best was nine hours, 47 minutes. It was the first time in 40 years we had finished above them without us winning the league, which perhaps indicated that they had fallen a little.

Unbelievably though, they were to trump us. They were to go and win the European Penalty Shoot-Out Cup. Of all the years for them to win the Champions League, they had to do it then. The nation shared in their joy, and took pride too, as they came from three goals down to take AC Milan to a penalty shoot-out. Evertonians on the other hand couldn't believe Serginho's penalty; he nearly hit the ducks in Stanley Park.

For weeks there had been a big debate over whether Liverpool should be allowed to defend the Champions League if they won it. Amazingly, nobody in charge of the game in England had put a rule in place that covered the possibility of a team finishing outside the top four but winning the Champions League.

There was a fear among some Evertonians - due to the wide variety of ways we had been excluded in the past - that we would be bounced out of the Champions League to make way for our neighbours. Thankfully that did not happen, but the theory persisted that the CIA would have a hand in the draw. And so we drew a team considered by some experts, given the seeding system, to be the most difficult opponents we could have faced.

Villarreal were a footballing fairytale. They had only entered the top flight of Spanish football seven years earlier, after having spent the previous 75 years in lower divisions and regional leagues, mainly the latter.

It was in 1998 that they made the big step up to the Primera Liga, with their first game against Real Madrid in the Bernabeu. The season ended in relegation. But businessman Fernando Roig, head of a flourishing ceramics company with factories in Villarreal, was enthused enough to take control of the club. Roig had plans, cunning plans. In the meantime, Villarreal went straight back up and consolidated as a top flight club over the next three seasons, finishing 7th, 15th and 15th.

Roig had been dismissed as a romantic when he said his aim was to see Villarreal play in Europe. It was a small town club in the shadow of Valencia 30 miles away. But they had sufficient humility to accept a place in the Intertoto Cup in the summer of 2003 and they won one of the three finals held in the tournament each year. This put them in the UEFA Cup for 2003-04, in which they reached the semi-finals, beating en route Trabzonspor, Torpedo Moscow, Galatasaray, Roma and Celtic. They also finished 8th in the league that season.

In 2004-05 they had reached the UEFA Cup quarter-finals then been among the chasing pack of clubs on the heels of Real Madrid and Barcelona. The competition in Spain for a UEFA Cup place was tough but Villarreal clinched one by finishing third.

Villarreal still had a relatively low profile but the media looked fondly on them, partly because they were underdogs who provided a good story but also because they could play some scintillating football.

Unable to compete in the transfer market with the big city clubs, Villarreal had turned to South America, signing a string of players from Argentina. Not every signing was a success but generally their hard running style and superb technical ability meant they adapted well to Spanish football. The club also picked up players in Europe who had not lived up to expectations, such as Argentine playmaker Juan Roman Riquelme, who had struggled to fit in at Barcelona, Uruguyan Diego Forlan, who had been branded a flop at Manchester United, and Argentine striker Luciano Figueroa, who had a dismal loan spell at Birmingham.

Roig also oversaw an increase in the capacity of the crowd from less than 10,000 to more than 20,000 and more than trebled the number of season ticket holders. He also placed a heavy emphasis on youth development.

Villarreal built a superb training complex that boasted eight pitches. Three were grass pitches, complete with floodlights, one of which was used for reserve team matches. There was also a building that included club offices, a gym, medical area, press room, hydro massage cabin, a coffee shop and an accommodation complex for more than 80 youth trainees. The first team was said to be just one of 40 various Villarreal sides that trained there. Sitting on the bench in the second leg against Everton were two of the first products of this scheme, Hector Font and Santi Cazorla.

How come this small town club had better training facilities than us, the big city club? Despite great plans for a new training and youth academy complex, it was proving to be slow in materialising. It seemed that the pressure to buy new players had been usurping money originally designated for new facilities. We could not afford both, it might be said.

The Villarreal coach was a Chilean, Manuel Pellegrini, who had been appointed in summer 2004. He fitted in well with Roig's masterplan because he knew Argentine football well from his time in charge of River Plate. Evertonians knew it was a tough draw but looked forward to seeing the Spaniards on Merseyside. As the big day approached, manager David Moyes summed up the sense of anticipation by declaring that it felt like Christmas Eve.

Neither club had played in the Champions League but we had a credible record in its predecessor, the European Cup, of played eight, won two, drawn five, lost one, scored 12, conceded six.

Before the game, Tony Heslop of the Ruleteros Society, devoted to developing links between the Goodison faithful and the Everton in Chile had presented Pellegrini with a copy of La Historia de Everton Football Club, an EFC history translated into Spanish. The Everton in Chile, well known to Pellegrini, had been set up a few months after Everton's 1909 trip to South America in which they beat an Argentine XI and a Uruguayan XI.

The ground was packed with Blues supporters in vociferous mood, creating an atmosphere worthy of the great European nights at Goodison. Remarkably, it was the first European Cup or Champions League game at Everton for 34 years. Heslop said: "An inspired performance involving a first half assault on their goal and a second half onslaught which lacked the final touch was matched by Villarreal's incisive attacking, courageous defending and a more effective Forlan than had ever played for Man United."

Villarreal had taken the lead through Figueroa but then came a glorious moment for James Beattie who stabbed the ball home for an equaliser. Just as the teams were about to go in level at half-time, José Joaquín Moreno Verdú flung himself at a cross. Before anyone could say his name, his header had hit the back of the net. Not only did it put Villarreal back in the lead, it also gave them a second, potentially crucial away goal. The second half was pulsating but goalless.

Evertonians left the ground disappointed at the defeat but almost unanimous in admiration for Villarreal's swift passing game. "That's how the game should be played," was the standard comment from supporters used to a Premiership diet of teams who gave priority to closing teams down rather than opening them up.

Still, there was everything to play for in the second leg. As Pellegrini said after the game: "Nothing has been decided yet. "We have another complicated match to get through and Everton have very resourceful players who can score at any point, and that would change everything."

As soon as the Champions League draw had been made, Evertonians had been booking up all available flights to anywhere in Spain within a 100-mile radius of Villarreal. With the town possessing only a few hotels, many Blues gravitated to Valencia for their pre-match aperitifs. Sitting in its squares, soaking up the sun, sipping their cappuchinos, and the very occasional beer, the blue male voice choirs serenaded each other with gravel-voiced gusto.

The club had only been given in the region of 1,700 tickets by Villarreal. This was something of a problem. Now that we seemed to be in Europe only every ten years, many supporters had vowed to go to every away game, no matter where it was played. Fortunately, enterprising Evertonians were able to capitalise on free market forces and an estimated 5,000 Blues obtained tickets for the game. It was an outpouring of exuberant Evertonianism, best illustrated by the DIY makeover that supporters gave to El Madrigal stadium. Blue and white flags hung almost everywhere. It seemed not like an away leg, but a neutral ground.

Among them was another Ruletero, John Shearon, who said: "Drawing Villarreal gave me the opportunity to take my family on a half-decent summer holiday. Having spent three weeks following the Everton in Chile earlier in the year, I had successfully negotiated with my partner for the summer holiday destination to be wherever the Champions League Third Round away leg was to be, although Kiev would have been pushing my luck."

Heslop said: "I will not forget the sight of thousands of Blues peacefully but noisily taking over main squares in Valencia and setting up Camp Goodison. I'll cherish too the harmony of Evertonians, Spaniards and a couple of Scots joining in massed sing songs before and after the game at the Villarreal Celtic Supporters Club, where our mementoes now hang alongside those of previous visitors."

The game kicked off with Villarreal again knocking the ball around sweetly, occasionally leaving us gasping, but generally the blue shirts matched them yard for yard. The first goal would be crucial so it was stomach-churningly disappointing when it came from Villarreal, especially as it took a cruel deflection off David Weir. There was one strange feature to the game. It was a Champions League tie but probably the most famous man on the pitch and the most recognisable was the referee, Pierluigi Collina from Italy. Somehow he had been deemed the best in the world. And with his distinctive appearance, he had become something of a celebrity.

Possibly the best known Everton player was 6ft 4ins tall Duncan Ferguson, seemingly the only handicapped footballer in the Premiership; whenever he jumps, a foul is given against him. I had sometimes wondered if Duncan might have been a natural at basketball, a sport much loved by Collina. Sadly, there was to be no natural affinity between the two men.

Was Duncan born too late? If only he had been playing in the Seventies when Everton had wingers like Dave Thomas and Ronnie Goodlass who would get to the goalline and send over crosses that met forwards as they leapt facing goal. Most of his headers for Everton since 1994 had been with his back to goal. In the Seventies he would also have enjoyed punk rock pogoing, something for which he had shown a talent at Goodison when complaining to referees.

Half-time came and went with Villarreal still 1-0 up on the night but steadily the Blues pressed their way back into the game. It was as Evertonians began to look at their watches, 20 minutes left, that we were awarded a free kick about 20 yards out. Mikel Arteta stepped up, took a look at the wall, glanced at the ball - a la Sheedy - then effortlessly stroked it into the roof of the net. Game on! It was 1-1 on the night and the Spaniards' aggregate lead was reduced to one goal.

Everton were in the ascendancy, just one more goal and we would take them to extra time. Of course, as any blue cynic would have told you, the game was set for a controversial refereeing decision. Would it go our way?

From a free kick the ball was curled into the Villarreal box and Duncan rose high above his markers - instinctively many Evertonians had risen with him, flexing their neck muscles - to execute a textbook header into the top of the net. But the perpetually startled-looking Collina had seen something in the penalty box not noticed by anyone else in the stadium, nor by anyone watching on television: it was the ghost of Bryan Hamilton. The Irishman was alive and well, but his ghost had arrived early, at the near post. Collina whistled and gave a free kick to the Spaniards. Everton players argued but, as the saying goes, referees can only give what they see - and Collina had seen an infringement by Hamilton. It was like something from the TV detective series Randall and Hopkirk (Deceased) - Randall could see the ghost of his deceased, white-suited partner Marty Hopkirk, played in the original series by Evertonian Kenneth Cope, and the problems he caused, but nobody else could. I am convinced this is why Collina suddenly retired from refereeing a few days later. Didn't you notice the haunted look on his face?

The goal should have put Everton 2-1 up on the night and made the aggregate score 3-3. Of course, against such a lively, attacking team as Villarreal, we might still have lost, but we could have accepted that. They did score another goal in the dying minutes but then we were desperately pushing forward in search of a goal to keep us in the tie. If Ferguson's goal had stood, we would have had the option of regrouping and waiting for extra time. But the record books state that Villarreal won both games 2-1 and the tie 4-2 on aggregate. It was off to the UEFA Cup party down the road.

25. MEDALS ALL ROUND

Dinamo Bucharest
UEFA Cup
2005-06

There was a good class of people in the UEFA Cup party. There were our old friends, Valerengen and Feyenoord, then there was sexy Seville and Mediterranean types such as Monaco and Marseille, and what a lot of Germans: Bayer Leverkusen, Stuttgart, Hamburg, Hertha Berlin and Mainz. Quite a few Italians too, Roma and Sampdoria caught the eye, and Portuguese clubs such as Vittoria Setubal. This could be fun. If we could just win our first round tie, there would be a group stage to enter which would give us at least a further four games in Europe. It would not be as lucrative as the Champions League, but it would help to raise the club's profile. And for the supporters, there could be some nice trips.

When Dinamo Bucharest was pulled out of the glass bowl from Ikea, there was a collective groan from Evertonians. We knew little about them, but previous World Cups had taught us that Romania produced some tricky footballers. And easyJet did not fly there, nor Ryanair, nor any other no-frills airline, which was ironic because Romania was a no-frills country. Perhaps our largely no-frills football might go down well there.

Everton had played Dinamo Bucharest once before, in North America during the 1961 International Soccer League. We had won 4-0, with two goals from Jimmy Gabriel and one apiece from Bobby Collins and Jimmy Fell.

Dinamo and their arch-rivals, Steaua Bucharest, had been political creations following the Second World War which had ended with the USA allowing the USSR to dominate eastern Europe. The Romanian regime's Interior Ministry - the secret police - formed Dinamo in 1948. A year earlier the Romanian army had set up its own football team ASA (Army Sport Association) which had later taken the name Steaua, which is English for The Star. Both were pre-dated by the capital city's third club, Rapid Bucharest, which had kicked off in 1923.

Dinamo had done the double in 2004 and played Manchester United in the UEFA Champions League qualifying round, losing 5-1 on aggregate, then they were knocked out of the UEFA Cup by Partizan Belgrade. In 2005, Dinamo narrowly lost the title race to Steaua, but had the consolation of winning the Cup. They would be no pushover; nor were we likely to be.

The chairman of Everton was now Bill Kenwright. He had put together a consortium, True Blue Holdings, which had acquired Peter Johnson's controlling stake in Everton in 2000. Kenwright did not have money left over to plough into the club, but he was convinced he was the right man to take the club forward and he had good reason to believe in himself. He had achieved much in life.

He had been brought up in post-war Liverpool, a fan of films and football. Probably due to his love of cinema, he was drawn to acting. His enthusiasm and self-confidence would have played no small part in helping him to pick up a variety of small TV roles before landing his first big break in 1968, a prominent part in Coronation Street as Betty Turpin's son, Gordon Clegg. But acting was not the only avenue he explored. There were his efforts as lead singer in Bill Kenwright and The Runaways. Despite the release in 1967 of singles such as I Want To Go Back There Again, chart success was elusive.

He eventually found his niche in theatre production where he honed his instinctive theatrical judgment and nascent negotiating skills. After a long slog which revealed a steely determination, Kenwright made himself a force in London's West End, putting on shows such as Joseph and the Technicolor Dreamcoat, Blood Brothers and Shirley Valentine. Following his success in the world of showbusiness, Kenwright prided himself on being able to "work the media" - important for a club no longer seen as one of the "Big Five" - and adept at striking deals, another vital asset in Premiership football. Not only would his skills be tested, but also his endurance and commitment although the latter was never in doubt due to his passion for Everton.

Under True Blue, plans were produced for a magnificent multi-use arena on the waterfront, to be built in partnership with the public sector, which would give the club a new stadium and an array of revenue streams. But the project failed to go ahead, for a variety of reasons, one being a lack of money.

Ironically, opera-loving Peter Moores' website revealed that his Foundation, set up in 1964, had now given away £104million, mainly for projects in music and the arts but also for education, health and the environment. Not surprisingly, he was knighted in 2003 for charitable services to the arts. Of course, an Evertonian would wish he would have given some to his father's favourite football club. However, from a non-enthusiast's perspective, football clubs were receiving huge amounts of money from Sky TV and merely spending it on transfer fees, agents' fees and £1million-plus salaries.

Perhaps we should have reminded him about the Everton opera. First performed in Teatro Nuovo, Naples, in 1824, Emilia di Liverpool was composed by Gaetano Donizetti. He had never visited Merseyside and had relied on descriptions received in letters from Italian emigrants passing through on their way to America. They may have been over-enthusiastic in their description of Everton Brow because the central character, the lovelorn Emilia, sought refuge in a hermitage in the mountains that surrounded the city. One can imagine that in the early 19th century Everton Brow looked even more bigger than it does today. It seems to have impressed Ferenc Puskas in the 1960s who talked of "the great river views from the hill near Everton". Perhaps the opera should be re-worked as Emilia di Everton, the tale of a dejected Toffee Lady who seeks refuge in a disused, brick lock-up with a round roof.

The Blues travelled to Bucharest on the back of a 1-0 home defeat by Portsmouth. Our league campaign had started badly with just one win from four games in which we had only scored one goal. Dinamo had warmed up however with a 6-0 win in their league over FCM Bacau.

Still, there were plenty of Blues keen to make the trip and planes had been chartered. But after a delay of several hours, around 160 supporters were called into a lounge at Liverpool Airport and told their flight had been cancelled - an air company had gone into liquidation. It was not a good omen.

The game in Bucharest began with Everton playing their usual pressing game. We were not at our best, but looked in no danger of being outclassed. It was a little surprising when the home side took the lead in the 27th minute, but a few minutes later Joseph Yobo headed an equaliser. After the interval the Romanians upped their tempo and took the lead with a fine goal in the 52nd minute when

Claudiu Iulian Niculescu skipped down the left wing and put over a great cross that was neatly turned in by Ianis Zicu.

The scoreline was not a huge problem but Dinamo then steadily gained in confidence, putting together some neat passing, as we increasingly looked leaden-footed. The warning signs were flashing before the Romanians scored their third, then their fourth. In flashes they played some great football that suggested they were boyhood fans of the legendary Gheorghe Hagi. The more optimistic Evertonians did their mental arithmetic and told the despondent that a 3-0 win at a packed Goodison was a distinct possibility which would put us through on the away goals rule. But on the stroke of full time, they scored another. Final score on the night was Dinamo Bucharest 5, Died-on-their-feet Everton 1.

On another night of the week, the Romanians' finishing might not have been so clinical and we could have been looking at, say, a two-goal deficit. But among Evertonians there was huge anger at the way the team had buckled. Given the optimism that had preceded the game, the disenchantment was understandable. But Evertonians had now been through so many new dawns that turned into thunderstorms, some felt they couldn't take any more. Quite a few were saying they had had enough. Sorry lads, but there's no escape; you can take the Evertonian out of Goodison but you can't take the Goodison out of the Evertonian.

Listen to Peter Hill who, approaching his 50th birthday, had decided a few months earlier that it was a good time to have a mid-life crisis and give up his job in Britain for as long as his money would last out. I asked him to explain.

He wrote: "I am spending six months leading an idyllic life on a tropical island called Koh Samui in the Gulf of Thailand. I am surrounded by palm trees, glorious beaches and the crystal-clear sea. I usually get up at noon and my only decisions are where to have breakfast and whether to have a massage or a swim. A good meal costs less than a quid. It would be perfect if only my mind did not keep wandering to the painful events 6,000 miles away at Goodison Park.

"In the Far East, nearly all Premiership matches are shown on satellite TV, so every weekend I go through the painful ritual of watching my beloved Blues sink further into the mire.

"What makes it worse is that the new expert analyst of the Singapore-based satellite channel Star Sport is one Les Ferdinand, who always scored against Everton in his playing career. Now he is torturing us with platitudes: 'Everton will struggle this season ... they over-performed last season.' You have heard them all already.

"Each day I forlornly head to internet cafes to share my frustrations with fellow Blues around the world. Usually there is a derisive email waiting for me from a former colleague who supports the European champions (it hurt to type those last two words). I am in paradise but it feels like hell."

Being an Evertonian is not like following other clubs where football is merely a welcome break from the pressures of everyday life. It's the other way round with us, the pressures of everyday life are a welcome break from being an Evertonian. But then, perhaps that is our own fault. We sing that we don't care what the red lot say, but we do allow ourselves to get wound up.

Dinamo Bucharest arrived on Merseyside for the second leg with confidence high after a 5-2 win over Rapid. Everton were bottom of the Premiership table. New signings Per Kroldrup and Andy Van Der Meyde were injured and yet to play a Premiership or European match for the Blues; Allesandro Pistone and Lee Carlsey, regulars last season, had long-term injuries, as did Gary Naysmith. James Beattie, signed in January for £6million, had been sidelined for the last five games but was hopeful of being on the subs bench. On the eve of the game, it emerged that summer signing Simon Davies was injured. Young James Vaughan might have been called up but he was out for weeks too. It was almost a whole team crocked.

David Moyes was coming in for criticism. But I shall be eternally grateful to the man. Before his arrival, we had become accustomed to finishing in the bottom half of the Premiership. It was as if staying up was the season's target. Moyes raised the bar, raised the level of ambition. If we had not won at an away ground since the Industrial Revolution, he expected that to change. And I loved the way he restored a cavalier element to Everton's play. If we needed goals in a game, he would fling on all the strikers he had sitting on the bench.

He had endeared himself to supporters from the day of his appointment by referring to Everton as "The People's Club" on Merseyside. In his first full season, working mainly with a squad of players he had inherited, the Blues finished seventh, narrowly missing out on a UEFA Cup spot. The next season was a dismal one. But in 2004-05 we held third place from September to Christmas before slipping to our true position in the order of things that season, fourth.

Debate had continued among supporters about the future of the club. Perhaps Everton may one day follow the Bundesliga model where clubs are owned by members - essentially the supporters. The precise management structure can vary, but most clubs have a supervisory board, elected by those members, which in turn appoints a management board who actually do the day-to-day running. Now that would be the People's Club. And if it works for Bayern Munich, surely it can work for Everton.

We approached the second leg against Dinamo, still hoping we could get through to the group stage. After all, it would not be over until the Toffee Lady had sang. Obviously we needed a bagful of goals. A big crowd would be a help. Following the poor start to the season, only 22,000 went through the turnstiles, but it was the noisy ones who had turned up and they dutifully cranked up the volume as if there were 22,000 tenors.

Everton swept into attacking mode and surged towards the Romanian goal time and time again, tackling any Bucharest player who had the effrontery to take possession of the ball, but the chances that we made were mainly going wide. Duncan Ferguson was the fulcrum of many of the attacks and it was from one of his knock-downs that Tim Cahill scored with a header on the half-hour. Could we get a second before half-time? No, but at least the Romanians failed to score an away goal during their occasional breakaways.

The second half saw Everton again pile on the pressure but the tempo did not seem to be quite so high. The Romanians were resolute in defence and looked increasingly assured as the game wore on. But even with 15 minutes left, there was still a glimmer of hope and the crowd was continuing to urge the Blues on. But in the final minutes of the game, the crowd's main concern was that Mikel Arteta would walk again. As he jumped for a header, he was the victim of a challenge so late it was in a different time-zone.

Beaten 5-2 on aggregate, the Everton team were applauded off the pitch. The supporters were pleased that Everton had given an all-out attacking display, with plenty of commitment. It's at times like this one can only wonder if Evertonians should be given medals; an OBE, denoting One Brilliant Evertonian. For those with the longest service, there could be a MBE, Mad, Brilliant Evertonian. If the club cannot give out these medals, they should sell them in the club shop.

Tony Heslop said: "Coming out of Goodison, I felt proud of the Blues overall, heartened by the crowd's display of loyalty to team and manager. And I felt sorry for the teenage Evertonians, not really old enough to appreciate the great times but old enough to suffer the setbacks and, yes, bad luck that is food and drink to an Evertonian."

Spookily, on the same night, the two teams in the competition whom we had played before in Europe, Valerengen and Feyenoord, were knocked out by the Bucharest clubs, Steaua and Rapid.

It did not take long for the snipers in the media to start taking potshots at Everton although there were several decent articles offering some reasoned analysis of our Euro failure. One came two days later in The Guardian from Kevin McCarra but even he described us as "a club of moderate prestige".

Listen here, mate. Everton is one of the greatest football clubs in the world. The greatness of a football club should not be measured solely in terms of trophies. If you do that, we are greater than Chelsea, with our nine championships to their two. The greatness of a football club has as much to do with its imprint on history, the passions it inspires, the loyalty it elicits and the hopes harboured for the future. There are many great football clubs but Everton has been the source of intense passion, lonesome loyalty and huge hope for longer than virtually all others. It's looking well for a 127-year-old, flawed but fantastic.

But the question remains: Why have we not done better in Europe? Some statistical analysis offers some possible answers.

Before 2005, we had been knocked out of Europe 10 times. Let's go through them: Dunfermline, by a one-goal margin; Inter Milan, by one goal; Manchester United, by one goal; Ujpest Dozsa, by two goals; Real Zaragoza, by one goal; Panathinaikos, on the away goal rule; AC Milan, by one goal; Dukla Prague, on the away goal rule; Feyenoord, by two goals in 1979, and by one goal in 1995.

The recurring theme is the close margin of defeat. On six out of ten occasions, we lost a two-legged tie by one goal; on two occasions, we lost on the away goal rule; twice we lost by two goals. Never were we hammered in those ties. Were we unlucky or just not quite good enough? Let's take another look:

Dunfermline: We claimed that their late winner was offside and then we had a last-gasp "equaliser" disallowed.
Inter Milan: We had a "goal" disallowed at Goodison.
Manchester United: Remember that ball which rolled along the United goalline, hit the post and spun into the goalkeeper's arms?
Ujpest Dozsa: Well beaten in Hungary.
Real Zaragoza: A melee involving several players broke out but only Johnny Morrissey was sent off, and we had to play the second half of the first leg with 10 men, during which time our opponents scored a crucial goal.
Panathinaikos: Big complaints over the refereeing in Greece, but really only ourselves to blame for failing to score at least two or three at home. Went out in the quarter-finals undefeated!
AC Milan: Had Mick Bernard sent off at Goodison. Big complaints over the refereeing in Italy, notably the Gary Jones penalty incident.
Dukla Prague: So close, so tight.
Feyenoord, 1979: Lost both games 1-0, but we didn't score so only ourselves to blame.
Feyenoord, 1995: Very close affair, but if you do not put the ball in the net, how can you win?

In search of more insight, let's look at our overall record in Europe. We have played 49 games, so the next one will be a milestone

50th. We have won 24, drawn 12 and lost 13, scored 75 goals and conceded 44.

Put another way, we have won half of our games, drawn a quarter and lost a quarter. We have conceded virtually a goal every game, which would not be bad but for the fact we have only scored 1.5 goals per game, or three goals in a two-legged tie. Perhaps this is the crux of the problem, not enough goals. We can blame referees and bad luck, but perhaps we have only ourselves to blame.

This goal-scoring problem is borne out further if we deduct the games against Icelandic and Irish opposition. No disrespect intended, of course, but the teams we played from these countries were composed of amateurs and part-timers. We played eight games, won seven, drawn one, scored 26 and conceded five.

If we consider just the games against teams from mainland Europe, and also the tie with Manchester United, we played 41, won 17, drawn 11, lost 13, scored 49 and conceded 39. Again, we conceded virtually a goal every game. But instead of 1.5 goals per game, we scored little more than one goal per game; in every six games, we scored a total of seven goals.

Our best goalscoring record came with the 1984-85 team which played nine, won seven, drew two, scored 16 and conceded two. Even then, our goalscoring record was not fantastic - an average of less than two goals per game. The 1970-71 team scored 12 goals in six games, an average of two a game, but nine of those were against Keflavik. In the other four games, we scored just three goals.

A huge number of goals were not required for success. Liverpool scored 139 goals in 278 games up to and including their European Cup semi-final in 1985, an average of two a game. But they scored on average 0.5 goal per game more than us, or an average of one more goal in each two-legged tie. So often, that one goal would have made the difference.

Arguably, this is borne out by comparing Liverpool eras. Under Bill Shankly, the Reds scored 114 goals in 65 games, an average of 1.75 goals and won one trophy in 10 years. Under Bob Paisley, they scored 130 goals in 57 games, an average of 2.28, and won four trophies in nine years.

Of course, there is a "chicken or the egg" argument here. Was our goalscoring in Europe record not better because of missed chances, and to a much lesser extent disallowed goals, or because we were not good enough generally to create more chances and to score more goals. Either way, I think we can put a lack of goals down as one reason for our relative failure in Europe.

For the record, our top scorers were: 6 - Fred Pickering; 5 - Andy Gray; 4 - Alan Ball, Joe Royle, Andy King, Graeme Sharp; 3 - Johnny Morrissey, Alex Young, Bob Latchford; 2 - Colin Harvey, Derek Temple, Brian Harris, Howard Kendall, Kevin Sheedy, Trevor Steven, Micky Walsh and the irrepressible Oggy (o.g.). Obviously, if Everton could have got into the group stages in 2005 of the Champions League or UEFA Cup, the top goalscorer position was up for grabs.

For those wondering who made the most appearances, the answer is: 19 - Brian Labone, Colin Harvey; 17 - Tommy Wright, Johnny Morrissey; 16 - Derek Temple; 15 - Jimmy Gabriel, 13 - Alex Young, Gordon West; 12 - Brian Harris, Dennis Stevens.

In discussing the club's record in Europe, we must remember the view of Labone who, reflecting on Everton's early ventures, said: "I do not think English football generally was up to the tactical expertise of the Europeans. I think they were much more ahead of us, certainly in the Sixties, although towards the end of the Sixties we became more aware."

Labone's perspective is underpinned by the fact that before 1968 only two English teams had won a European trophy, Spurs and West Ham, in the Cup Winners Cup. Then a string of English clubs won their first European trophy: 1968 - Manchester United (European Cup) and Leeds (Inter Cities Fairs Cup); 1969 - Newcastle (Inter Cities Fairs Cup); 1970 - Manchester City (Cup Winners Cup) and Arsenal (Inter Cities Fairs Cup); 1971 - Chelsea (Cup Winners Cup); 1973 - Liverpool (UEFA Cup); 1979 - Nottingham Forest (European Cup); 1981 - Ipswich (UEFA Cup); 1982 - Aston Villa (European Cup).

The superstitious may have noted who was the 13th English club to win a European trophy, and that we then found ourselves banned. While that the 5-1 drubbing in Bucharest, easily our heaviest in Europe, was our 13th defeat in European competition, which came in the 13th European competition we had entered, although it was our 12th season in Europe (two competitions in one season),

Our next season in Europe will be our 13th, but that did not do Liverpool any harm. It was in their 13th season in Europe that they won their first European Cup.

We can hope for better luck in the future, but probably the better thing to do is try and make our own luck. At the end of the day, what Everton Football Club has achieved is down to its own efforts. What it has not achieved is down to us too, nobody else. We get knocked down, we get up again. There is everything to play for in the future. And if Evertonians can pull together and stick together, everything is achievable. In any case, it's only a game, and the ball is round. Come on you Blues!

BIBLIOGRAPHY

A Strange Kind Of Glory, Sir Matt Busby and Manchester United, by Eamon Dunphy, published in 1991 by William Heinemann Ltd.

Dixie Dean, The Story Of A Goalscoring Legend, by Nick Walsh, published in 1977 by Pan Books.

Everton: A Complete Record 1878-1985, by Ian Ross and Gordon Smailes, published in 1985 by Breedon Books.

Everton Greats, by Jon Berman and Malcolm Done, published in 1997 by Mainstream; revised, 2003.

Everton, Player by Player, by Ivan Ponting, published in 1992 by Guinness Publishing.

Everton, The School of Science, by James Corbett, published in 2003 by Macmillan.

Football & Fortunes, The Inside Story Of Littlewoods Pools, 1923-2003, edited by Phil Reed, published in 2003 for Littlewoods Promotions by Brahm Limited.

History of the Everton Football Club, 1878-1928, by Thomas Keates, published in 1929 by Thomas Brakell and reproduced in 1998 by Desert Island Books.

Liverpool In Europe, by Stephen F. Kelly, published in 1992 by Collins Willow.

Never Say Dai, by Dai Davies, published in 1986 by Siop Y Siswrn.

Puskas on Puskas, edited by Rogan Taylor and Klara Jamrich, published in 1998 by Robson Books.

The Beautiful Game? Searching For The Soul Of Football, by David Conn, published in 2004 by Yellow Jersey Press.

The King, Denis Law, published in 2003 by Bantam Press.

The Blues And I, by Kevin Ratcliffe, published in 1988 by George Weidenfeld & Nicolson.

The Essential History Of Everton, by Mark Platt, published in 2000 by Headline Book Publishing.

Toffee Pages, The Post-War Years, by David France, published in 1997 by Skript Design & Publishing.

Tor! The Story Of German Football by Ulrich Hesse-Lichtenberger, published in 2002 by WSC Books Ltd.

Winners & Losers, by Stefan Szymanski and Tim Kuypers, published in 1999 by Penguin Group.

www.rsssf.com